THE WAY TO THE STARS

SERMONS FOR TODAY

THE WAY TO THE STARS

Sermons for the Space Age

Leonard Barnett

LONDON
EPWORTH PRESS

SBN 7162 0174 7

Printed in Great Britain at the St Ann's Press
Park Road, Altrincham

CONTENTS

ACKNOWLEDGEMENTS

The author is grateful to Collins Publishers for permission to quote from *The Neophiliacs* by Clifford Booker. All Bible references are from the *New English Bible* unless otherwise stated.

1) By What Authority?

SOME time ago, at a Cambridge hotel, a rowdy and frightening student demonstration took place against the Greek military régime. There was a lot of noise, a good deal of damage done to the hotel lawn and windows, and a policeman injured. A few days later, at a widely publicized trial, six students, selected from the many present at the incident, were sent to gaol for periods of nine to eighteen months. Two went to Borstal; and two were recommended for deportation back to their home countries of South Africa and Brazil.

I did my best to study the reports of the case. I began by being prejudiced, I confess, in favour of the Cambridge townsfolk dining at the hotel who were badly scared by the affair. I have a rooted objection to intimidation of anybody by anybody, at all times. I still think what was done was indefensible and disgraceful. But I think what was done in court at Cambridge was monstrous. I protest against it. The process by which the defendants were selected for trial, the type and force of the evidence against them, the inevitable political overtones of the trial, and what I will call the cruelty of the sentences, make me as a Christian advocate want to echo an ages-old question, sharply posed in every age by men challenged and outraged by what they have seen going on around them.

By what authority are you acting like this? Who gave you this authority? You may well wish, as I did, to ask it of the rioting students. You may want to ask it now of their judge.

We heard the same questions echoed a few minutes ago, in this service; echoing over the centuries, from the Temple in Jerusalem, as Jesus faced his angry critics.

'Your credentials!' they demanded, scandalized. 'By what authority are you acting like this? Who gave you this authority?'[1]

Short, sharp, simple questions. They take us to the heart of things if you care to make the journey. The simplest questions are often the most deceptive. Square up to them, tackle them seriously, and there's no knowing what you may discover.

What right have you got to behave this way? We've asked the question ourselves when we thought we were clearly entitled to do. We have spoken it aloud. We have muttered it under our breath, when we were afraid of being counter-charged and routed. We have asked it silently, nursing some secret sense of shame or rage or horror, as we looked round on the world of our day, in which authority seems so often to have run amok.

Here, in the temple, the questioners ought to have known better. Deep down, they knew perfectly well what the answer was. The same scene had been played out again and again, in the course of their history. Only the time and place, and the players, had changed. The script had been written, and played for real, again and again. The chief priests and elders really should have held their peace.

Let's reconstruct one of those scenes now. We began to recollect it a few minutes ago, as we read the Old Testament scriptures.

We take a giant stride back, almost eight centuries before that confrontation between Jesus and his critics in the temple at Jerusalem. The scene is an earlier shrine, famous—or infamous; Bethel: centre of a prosperous

[1] Matt. 21:23.

2

community. Trade boomed. The land was at peace. Money flowed—but into the pockets of the few. Wealth and poverty rubbed shoulders. The moneyed class flaunted their luxury. The destitute clustered hard by in their pitiful hovels.

Officially, religion flourished. Outwardly, it was dedicated to the worship of Jehovah. Rite and ritual, feast and festival, tithe and sabbath observance were meticulously observed. The priests carried out their duties faithfully. Splendid decorum reigned.

There was another side to the picture; a sick aspect; ugly; evil.

It was ignored by the Establishment. But it burned into the brain of an uncouth, unlettered herdsman, Amos, a few miles away with his sheep on the barren mountainside at Tekoa. He was an obscure nobody, without scholarship, pretension or credential. He had no sacred book to support him: no tradition to buttress his arguments.

All he knew with blazing certainty was that what went on both in temple and market place was a blasphemy, an affront to the God with whom he knew he was in communion, with whom he felt himself at one. His God was the Great Original of all truth and righteousness, of mercy and judgement.

Amos was arrested by what those in power ignored. He could not possibly ignore it. He saw humanity being forgotten; men's rights, as children of a righteous loving, merciful God, trampled on by other men who, deep down, denied God: whose outward religion was shadow but no substance, solemn activity but no loving action.

He saw honest men ground into the dust, sold callously as debtors, for a song. The price of a pair of shoes would buy such a man. He saw greedy merchants short measuring grain and overweighting precious metal, tilting the scales fraudulently. He saw the opulent debauching themselves with other men's money. He saw, as everyone could with

3

eyes to see, the degradation that went on in the so-called house of God, in which girls dedicated to the task offered their bodies to all comers and thought, with their clients, they did God service as they lay together. A man and his son would visit the same girl. The soul of Amos was seared by it all. Israel's violent warring neighbours were barbarous enough, in all conscience. He was not blind to their cruelties. But the crimes of civilization were no less hideous. They were an outrage against all he knew God to be, all he knew God demanded of men: *all* men.

There stirred within him a new, strange compulsion: a message of fire: the word of God. He listened and obeyed the inner summons. He found himself possessed of a power, a strength, a spirit which was not to be gainsaid. He left his flock, and strode into the shrine at Bethel. There he lifted up his voice and declared the judgement of God on the evil—the evil of brazen lovelessness—God had given him eyes to recognize and reject.

And—just as it happened eight centuries later—he set the Establishment by the ears. 'The country cannot tolerate what he is saying!' exclaimed the priest of Bethel to the king. And to Amos he shouted—'Be off with you!'

But Amos could not be silenced.

'I am no prophet', he said, 'nor am I a prophet's son; I am a herdsman and a dresser of sycomore-figs. But the Lord took me as I followed the flock and said to me, "Go and prophesy to my people Israel." . . . Now these are the words of the Lord.'[1]

His words rang true. They were words of authority: the word of God, no less. He spoke of God holding up as it were a plumb-line to Israel, and finding the nation not straight and true, but bowed and bent by evil—by injustice, cruelty, greed, self-love, self-indulgency, pride, sloth. The nation was like an over-ripe basket of fruit, apparently blooming, but soft to the touch, rotten within.

[1] Amos 7:14–16

4

Let justice roll on like a river, he thundered,
And righteousness like an ever-flowing stream.
Seek good and not evil,
 that you may live,
that the Lord the God of Hosts may be firmly on your side,
 as you say he is.
Hate evil and love good;
 enthrone justice in the courts.[1]

It was a word for all seasons; a word of authority; then; and now. A radical, non-conformist word, seeking to put down the mighty from their thrones and exalt them of low degree.

It was backed by no earthly authority: but it penetrated the heart and conscience of his fellows. Amos, and others like him, declared the truth and authority of God himself: whose love is as great as his power, and neither knows measure nor end; and is for you, now, likewise to accept and believe, and live by: at all costs.

Look, and look again, carefully, at this ancient encounter. It will lead you to the heart of the theme we are pursuing: to the first of three great facts concerning this over-arching theme of authority.

And that is . . . ?

That life is a battleground: where an immemorial, life-and-death struggle is forever fought; as urgent today as it was yesterday, and will be tomorrow—and all our tomorrows.

At the encounter at Bethel we see just one epic moment —the Bible relates a thousand such—in the eternal warfare between good and evil, light and darkness, love and self-love. There, plain and stark, we see symbolized, the collision between the authority of God—the authority of goodness and love—and the self-brandished authority of man, the rebel, headstrong, proud, self-centred, but

[1] Amos 5:24; 14–15

who can relinquish his role if he wishes; can pay the price of obedience; and become God's ally instead of his enemy; his spokesman; his champion.

From personal communion with God himself, Amos derived the courage, the vision, the ability he needed to take in, then pass on, the message. It was a blazingly clear directive. Men, as sons of the Father, were to honour, not dishonour each other; to reverence, not ravage, ministering to each other's good, not contriving each other's downfall. To oppress, to persecute, to exploit and degrade, was a blasphemy, a denial of the truth lying at the very heart of reality. It was to deny God: to live in darkness.

The authority Amos wielded was shared with other men of his own age and those that followed. They felt and knew what he did. They too could not keep silent. They had to speak and live the truth or die in the attempt: the truth that God was goodness and love, and demanded of men that, made in his image, they reflected him in their lives, to his glory and theirs. They could not remain disobedient to the heavenly vision. They had no option having seen and heard but to proclaim it; and they did.

These men—Amos, Hosea, Micah, Isaiah, and the rest of the great Old Testament prophets—were a new breed; men of invincible authority; men of God indeed. They might be hunted, stoned, flung into loathsome dungeons, tormented, killed; they could not be silenced while they had breath to declare with authority the timeless truth God had made known to them. Their message struck home to heart and conscience on its own self-evident merit. No human authority could either enforce it or destroy it. They represented an enormous, vital break through in the story of God's traffic with men, and in the story of humanity. The whole world lies in debt to these giant souls, whose insight and fidelity lie at the very heart of whatever is best in the human story from then until now.

6

So: what more completely apt than that we should find the second towering fact of life to which we want to bear witness, in the appearance of the Master of life, Jesus of Nazareth, of whom men unhesitatingly said, witnessing his words and works in awe and wonder, that he was assuredly a prophet, standing in the great line of succession of those who bore about with them the authority of God.

What more completely apt than that he should have announced his mission, in fact, at synagogue in his own home town, by reading a majestic, compassionate word from one of the very greatest of the seers of old—Isaiah?

Recall what happened.

Jesus, 'armed with the power of the Spirit', as Luke significantly says, returned to Galilee, entered Nazareth, and read out to the assembled congregation:

> *The Spirit of the Lord is upon me because he has*
> *anointed me;*
>
> *he has sent me to announce good news to the poor,*
> *to proclaim release for prisoners and recovery of*
> *sight for the blind;*
>
> *to let the broken victims go free . . .'*[1]

And what followed?

He declared the loving authority of God—and collided with the self-love of man.

He spelled out in plain language, proving his case by reference to sacred stories of their race which over the years his people had come to venerate and indeed foolishly idolize, just what Isaiah had meant to imply. The God in whose house they were even then worshipping was bidding his chosen race break down the centuries-old barriers they had so firmly, solemnly erected between Jew and Gentile. God had no favourites. His goodwill extended to all mankind. Pride in race and blood mattered not at all to him. Their holy destiny was to share God's blessings, his liberating truth, his sovereign law of love to all men,

[1] Luke 4:18

with all mankind. This was what they had indeed been chosen of God to do.

And then . . . ?

By what authority . . .? they demanded to know. Not in so many words, but in the clearest possible sense. They were not merely annoyed. They were infuriated; they displayed all the signs of hard selfish men called upon to demolish their pride, to share their power and privilege with the lowliest. They rose up, threw him out of the synagogue, and would have lynched him.

Do you remember the clear witness Mark bears to this same truth about the Son of Man in the opening chapter of his own—and earliest—account of the life of Jesus? How he went into the lakeside synagogue at Capernaum, and began to teach?

'The people were astounded at his teaching,' says Mark, 'for, unlike the doctors of the law, he taught with a note of authority'. It was direct, convincing, totally unlike the deathly tedium of the usual harangues to which the congregation listened, Sabbath by dreary Sabbath, from rabbis everlastingly quoting each other for mutual support.

On this memorable occasion, Jesus was interrupted by the shrieking voice of a feeble minded member of the congregation. Again his uncanny authority was seen. His healing rejoinder was the bestowal of serenity, swift and startling, on this tormented mind. 'They were all dumbfounded and began to ask one another, "What is this? A new kind of teaching! He speaks with authority. When he gives orders, even the unclean spirits submit." The news spread rapidly . . .'[1]

No wonder.

And so it continued. Wherever he went, whatever he did, whatever he said, his words and works, his life and mission, spoke with exactly the same power, exactly the

[1] Mark 1:27–28

8

same authority, as had the prophets of old. Indeed, it was commonly said that he was in fact one of those prophets, returned to earth again. Like them, he had no credentials, no influential background, no support group to speak of. His authority came from within. Sometimes, it was seen and heard as he used the sacred scriptures which had become, since the days of Amos, so immeasurably precious but so blindly authoritative, so harshly binding upon the Jews. This man unbelievably dared to set his own authority over against even the authority of the sacred book, as absolute. 'You have heard it said of old', he would tell them, 'but what *I* say is . . .'

And what followed was truth of a sort never heard before, but so plain, so utterly convincing, it remained indelibly printed on their minds and hearts. They might fail to accept it. They could not fail to remember it.

Always, it was the word of love, of healing, of help, of reconciliation: the word of authority which insisted on forgiveness, free and unlimited; utter readiness to open heart and hand to everyman in need, always. He spoke tenderly, sternly, plainly. The common people heard him gladly. He spoke with the clarity of a child and the profundity of a seer. His constant theme was one mastertruth—that all were children of the heavenly Father; and that giving and forgiving, in love and pure goodness, they should create his commonwealth, his new society, his kingdom; a kingdom built in obedience to the first and last law of love.

At the end of his life, this same obedience had led him directly to the situation in which they flung the question to him. A day or two before, he had engineered a classic demonstration, he and his rabble of peasant followers. He had ridden into the capital, near Passover, laying clear deliberate claim to the fulfilment of an ancient prophecy; identifying himself with the gentle king believed of old to be coming one day to claim his kingdom; not on a prancing charger, but seated meekly on an ass, the foal of a beast of burden.

It was the same love again which had led him only a day later to act out anything but a gentle role, erupting into the temple like a hurricane, sending flying the stalls at which money changers and vendors were cheating and extorting; hurling condemnation at them as men who had fouled a holy place into the likeness of a robbers' cave.

By what authority . . . are you acting like this? they raged.

But they knew, in their heart of hearts.

This man was a prophet—but more than a prophet.

He said he was the Way, the Truth, and Life itself. He spoke for God. He was filled with God. In a special, unique, self-evident sense, he was God's Son. Men, he said calmly, were summoned to learn of him, follow him, indeed lose their lives for his sake, in order to find their true selves; and God.

He symbolized in his whole life—not fitfully, not on one dramatic occasion, but throughout his whole ministry—the authority and the power of perfect goodness and love. The Prophets had been bright and shining lights. He was—and is—the Light of the world; shining from everlasting to everlasting.

His whole life, and supremely his death, spoke to men—and still speaks, today as yesterday the same—of God's goodness and love; ready to descend into the worst hell of suffering rather than deny itself. He stood invested with the authority with which, from then to now, God has summoned men in turn to be invested; the same redemptive authority of sacrificial love and goodness.

And this brings us to the third and final fact we have to proclaim.

And that is . . .?

That the battle of authority, of good against evil, still rages—and will, until the kingdoms of this world are

10

dissolved and become the kingdom of Christ; that God moreover still summons men to stretch out hands of penitence, faith and obedience to him, as he speaks in Christ. He invests such men with the same Godly authority, the same divine bestowal of self-sacrificial love and goodness that Amos discerned, and Christ knew in full glorious measure.

Men still do respond.

The battle still rages. Today, as yesterday the same, it inflicts appalling wounds upon a riven world since, in every age, everyman must make his own journey of faith and obedience to God's reign of goodness and truth. And any age may slip back headlong into the abyss. The world is not travelling on an escalator to the Kingdom. It is a personal ascent, for one and all. And it may be abandoned.

Come in mind and imagination for a moment, to another court of law—so-called—in one of the two most powerful nations on earth.

At the rear of the court is a plain van.

In the dock is a gifted writer, an intellectual, who will not silence either tongue or pen but has ventured to plead the cause of elementary human freedom and dignity, in opposition to a soulless State where human rights are strictly expendable.

This State has moved on from the crudity of simple execution of its dissidents. That policy is apt to spoil the image. Now, a subtler devilry has taken over. No honourable verdict of treason against this man. He, the sanest man in the court, is found criminally insane. The plain van whisks him away to a living tomb within the high walls of a mental institution, in which his tormentors intend that proud spirit and gifted mind to be steadily broken and destroyed to the level of the poor human hulks he is now penned with night and day.

There are many such prisoners, in Russia, today.

Or imagine, if you can stomach the thought, a dreadful

gaol in Brazil, where priests and nuns, not to mention ordinary political suspects, are confined; in which they are coolly, calculatingly subject to the most frightful sophisticated tortures the perverted minds of pitiless men can devise, to extort information, and to discourage others from challenging a régime, corrupt and evil almost beyond belief—in which terrorism is an act of policy, agony a tool of government.

(Or it might be Greece . . . which was why the students rioted, at Cambridge, you remember.)

Or again: here is a sad little convoy—one of many, over the years—somewhere in Southern Africa, piled with the pitiful possessions of a group of African families, abruptly uprooted from the place where they have lived for generations. The area which has been home has been declared suitable only for Europeans. The law has said so. The law is enforced. The black exodus begins, to an alien site, where they must start, from scratch, to create a tolerable community . . . somehow . . .

By what authority . . .? we cry.

The battle rages still. No man is an island. We need ask now less than ever, for whom the bell tolls. A Russian state asylum, a Brazilian gaol, a bleak windswept settlement on the veldt, an Ulster family staring in terror at their blazing home, two heart-broken parents coping with a drug addict son, or helping their daughter to face her pregnancy—or an abortion . . . or a million homes in which people create private hell for others through iron-hard selfishness, all these alike are parts of the maine of John Donne's world, shrunk to a neighbourhood; tokens one and all of the immemorial universal strife, in which ordinary men and women need now as much as ever to be invested with the authority of God, bespeaking a new power, greater still than the malignance of evil.

And men still do respond. The summons is heard. Where sin abounds, grace ever seeks to abound still more. The powers of darkness cannot extinguish the light that burns on in the hearts of men; the light of life; the radiance of the Holy Spirit forever seeking to invade and inly armour the soldiers of the living Christ.

I think again today, for instance, of that gifted, up-and-coming Boston Ph.D., in his late twenties, a middle class minister of the Gospel on the threshold of a successful, popular ministry in a thriving American church: suddenly summoned to put on the whole armour of God and stand invested in his authority and face the tyranny of evil in blatant form less than twenty years ago in an undistinguished (until then) Deep Southern town. A town, it was, in which the Establishment—the authority of self and pride—still decreed that multitudes were degraded daily in the ordinary relationships of community life; even down to the matter for instance of public transport. Segregation laws decreed that whites sat at the front of buses, blacks at the rear. Negroes were not allowed so much as to pass down the central aisle from front to back after paying their fare. They must dismount again, walk back, and board a second time. It was a traditional amusement to drive away before the coloured passenger had reached the step a second time.

You will recall the now famous story, I think; of the way in which, back in 1955, the town of Montgomery, Alabama, found a battle on its hands; a symbolic battle—the authority of sad, bad, tradition against the living word of God, the authority of goodness, truth and love. It sounded in the ears of a band of Christian brothers resolved once for all to stand and walk—literally—with dignity, patience, and unconquerable good will . . . until wrong was righted.

Their resolve invited derision. What real power had the black masses of Montgomery? What possible hope of success, against the entrenched, powerful, financial

13

interests of the bus company bitterly resolved to maintain traditional white supremacy?

I like to recall that quiet meeting, one fateful afternoon, as a group of committed men looked to the talented dynamic young minister in their midst, and asked him to become their appointed leader in the crusade. He knew full well that, if he agreed, as their spokesman he would draw down upon his head the fury and the hatred of the white Establishment. He would have to live dangerously. Tranquillity and security would cease.

'I don't mind,' said the young man diffidently. 'Somebody has to do it, and if you think I can, I will serve.'[1]

No shrill trumpet suddenly sounded in that small quiet room . . . no fire from heaven . . . no tongues of flame . . . any more than when Amos, musing silently among his sheep, sensed the summons of God. All the same, it was the moment of truth. The vision cleared; the summons came; the authority was accepted—conferred by men, created by God—authority to go ahead and give direction—the prime role of any leader.

It was the start of one of the more unforgettable chapters in the history of twentieth century Christian witness. The long drawn out, amazingly disciplined, sacrificial, non-violent campaign of the Montgomery bus boycott, ending in final dramatic victory, captured the world's imagination and cracked open the evil structure of social segregation in the Deep South.

Martin Luther King began to take his place, that day, with Luther and Wesley, William Carey, William Booth, Mary Slessor, Albert Schweitzer, Temple Gairdner and C. T. Studd, Martin Niemoller, Kagawa, Bishop Azariah and Albert Luthuli and so many more (of whom the world has never been worthy) who have shown their fellow disciples and the whole world, that the real battle

---

[1] Coretta Scott King, *My Life with Martin Luther King*, Hodder and Stoughton.

14

of life is still the Lord's: that it is not by man's power or brute force but by God's Spirit within a man, that the day of righteousness will ever dawn, and the powers of darkness be put to flight.

He also signed his own death warrant, that day in Alabama; as his Lord had done, so many centuries earlier, proclaiming the self-same authority of the Father, full of grace and truth.

The next twelve years were years of trial and torment, tension and travail; years of sacrifice, pain, anxiety: years of bitterest hatred and at times bleak hostility even, alas, from fellow Christians. But every rebuff was met with rocklike, Christlike refusal to hate in return. Martin Luther King met rage with meekness: constant threats and menace, with Christ-inspired grace and gallantry, serenity and steadfastness. It is not the duration of life, but its intensity, that matters, he said. The whole world knows the story of this man of authority, as he carried the burden, steadily and unafraid, of a man of God marked to die; a latter-day apostle dedicated to the cause of a non-violent, reconciled and reconciling world, in which the cruel barriers of pride and prejudice should one day be totally dismantled. He left behind an undying, indelible testimony, when finally that shot from the shadows came. Not one, but countless confrontations of Christlike, steadfast love with brazen, bitter evil, marked those years. They were years of battle; in which one man, and his no less faithful friends, yoked together by a common bond of allegiance to a suffering and risen Christ, in whose life and strength they stood invested with the self-evident authority of God's goodness and love, stood forth at once invincible and wholly vulnerable. *By whose authority?* his enemies roared in fury at him, again and again. But they, like Jesus' foes, knew the answer.

I name this man as one who symbolizes the role we too are to play. God, in Christ, still calls men to play the role of king; in two senses. They will suffer, and die. But dying, they live.

Martin Luther King, and all others, a few known, the vast multitude recorded only in the Book of Life, remind me of those eleven men, ordinary and very frail, whom Matthew pictures as gathered, at the last, on a mountain top in Galilee; there to fall in homage before their risen Lord—'though some', Matthew adds comfortingly, 'were doubtful'.

'Jesus then came up and spoke to them . . . "Full authority in heaven and on earth has been committed to me. Go forth therefore and make all nations my disciples . . . And be assured, I am with you always, to the end of time".'[1]

It was barely a month or two after that these men were facing the very authority—the Jewish Council—which had arraigned their Lord such a short time ago. Their new-found confidence, their astonishing authority, baffled their critics, as that of Jesus had done. Some Council members were for executing them out of hand. But wise Gamaliel, you remember, advised caution. 'If this idea of theirs is of human origin,' he said, 'it will collapse; but if it is from God, you will never be able to put them down.'[2] The Council took his advice, the apostles were flogged, ordered to give up speaking in the name of Jesus, and flung out. They went home bruised and bloody—but rejoicing they had been found worthy to suffer indignity for the sake of the Name. And every day they went steadily on with their teaching . . . telling the good news of Jesus . . .

Dressed, not in a little brief manmade authority, but in the 'full authority' of the risen Christ; men possessed of the Holy Spirit of God: eternal, unchangeable.

Like us . . . ?

[1] Matt. 28:18–20   [2] Acts 5:38

2) The Way to the Stars

WHEN Neil Armstrong climbed steadily down the nine rungs of the most famous ladder in history, he pulled the ring which activated a TV camera—itself a marvel of miniaturization, ten inches by six, requiring only the power you'd need for a fairy light on a Christmas tree—and, moments later, the vast audience back on earth saw him take what he so truly said was 'one small step for man, one giant leap for mankind'. Things would never be the same again. Men had taken, at last, the way to the stars.

How did you react, not only as a fellow human being, but as a Christian?

I take it, of course, you *did* react! For a Christian to shrug his shoulders and admit that he hadn't any feelings one way or another about this epoch-making journey, this unique achievement, would be a confession indeed.

Many people have freely offered us the benefit of their own opinions; including the Astronomer Royal, Sir Richard Woolley. Even as the moon men were preparing for their final descent to the lunar surface, he was being quoted as unrepentantly standing by an earlier assessment of the whole programme of space exploration, and in particular the effort to put a man on the moon, as 'utter bilge'. Glorious bilge, he said, maybe; a magnificent brave adventure. But not to be put into the category of other epics like North Pole tracking and climbing Everest; since the cost of mounting the operation, and the insignificant scientific results achieved, were so vastly different.

Is this your considered Christian reaction? That to put a man on the moon and bring him safely home again, and now to initiate far bigger, more ambitious space voyages still is, at best, an exciting enterprise, but basically a fantastically expensive irrelevance, a diversion without real meaning or significance?

If so, I think I know how you feel.

At the same time, as a fellow Christian, I repudiate your viewpoint almost entirely. I'd like to suggest a very different one.

It can be summed up in a pithy phrase from Paul's first letter to his friends at Corinth, chapter three, verse nine. 'In this work,' he says, 'we work with God.'[1]

What's more, I believe that not a few of that remarkable new breed of men, the American astronauts (and for all I know, some of their Russian colleagues as well) might well be prepared to go along with Paul's succinct assertion, as summing up what they themselves feel about the daring mission to which they have dedicated life and limb no less specifically, sacrificially, than any Christian missionary ever did embarking for alien shores. Voyaging into space, to be sure, is a radically different undertaking, from the outside. Nonetheless, I believe that in the deepest sense, and certainly any Christian helping to mount this most spectacular scientific operation of all time, is entitled to say with sense and fidelity—in this work we too work with God. At root, it is both his undertaking and ours. It is a joint enterprise.

What is more, I believe it not just rather desirable that Christians should see and gladly embrace this viewpoint. I hold it to be vital. This is the simple justification for what I want to say in this sermon for today.

I am encouraged, and I hope you are too, by the sort of slight but real evidence already laid, suggesting that some

[1] J. B. Phillips' translation.

18

of the new space age *corps d'élite* share this viewpoint to an extent. You recall the revealing moment at which an earlier Apollo crew, girdling the moon at Christmas, 1968, thought fit to read at the moment a snatch of the majestic Genesis creation narrative. You may also have read Edwin Aldrin's simple, unselfconscious account of what must surely have been the most extraordinary piece of Extra-Vehicular Activity to take place on the lunar surface. Aldrin, a practising Christian, requested an air-to-ground silence for a spell, during which he took Communion from a miniature chalice. When every second, every ounce, was of vast importance, such an event speaks for itself. Cynics, of course, may sneer at such actions and see in them nothing but religious American schmaltz. I think they are wrong.

I believe, on the contrary, that here we find genuine sentiment, not sentimentality, and sentiment of a deeply significant sort. They are tokens of the attitude, the faith of a Christian along the way to the stars, which I am eager to encourage. To me, they integrate completely with the impression one gains repeatedly, listening to those amazingly calm, controlled voices from both outer space and Mission Control. They do not sound like the voices of latter day Frankensteins. They are not shrill, neurotic. Neither are they bombastic, arrogant. They are understandably exultant, at times. They have every right to be. But they seem to me to be patently the voices of men not only possessed of brilliant expertise and justifiable confidence, but also, and equally importantly, men of genuine humility, aware that they are treading the rim of awesome mysteries—the mysteries of what has rightly been called, from one vantage point, the violent universe, but which is also serenely controlled, dependable, planned and patterned. These men of whom I speak convey an impression, at any rate, rightly or wrongly, that they would not object to being described as co-workers with, rather than impious intruders upon, the realm of whatever Supreme Intelligence may rule the heavens and all that is therein.

This surmise, in fact, agrees well with the remarkable testimony of Norman Mailer's vivid firsthand account of life at NASA long before and during the Apollo mission. Few Americans are less naive, more ruthlessly contemptuous of the phoney, than Mailer. What he so brilliantly, percipiently writes is therefore all the more astonishing. It offers the clearest impression that the men behind the moonshot, high and low, view and experience their work as belonging to heaven as well as earth. It infects them with attitudes unmistakably humble, gentle, happy, deeply (one almost said 'divinely') fulfilled; behaving, to use Mailer's virtually incredible words, as 'true Christians'. And that from the author of *The Naked and the Dead*!

One thing I am sure about. Paul would not object to us taking this word of his and using it in this uncommon context. On the contrary, I believe he would be deeply in harmony with the view I want to expound. He would be as intensely interested and concerned, as a Christian, in our first tentative steps to the stars, as I hope you are. He too, like us, would be seeking to interpret them, to use his own favourite phrase, 'in Christ'; through whom, as he insisted two thousand years ago, God chose to reconcile the whole universe to himself.

Now: how can we get to grips with the theme?

By pondering a blunt, basic, wellworn Bible question; in the light of the bold—indeed startling—comment which follows it.

You remember it well. It comes in a psalm that could have been written indeed for the space age. The question emerged into the mind of the writer as he pondered the haunting mystery of the heavens, the work of God's fingers; the moon and the stars as established by him.

'*What is man*', he mused, '*that thou art mindful of him, and the son of man that thou dost care for him?*'

Then the reflection, so prophetic in the light of twentieth century technology.

'*Yet thou hast made him little less than God, and dost crown him with glory and honour. Thou hast given him dominion over the works of thy hands; thou hast put all things under his feet . . .*'[1]

The question, and the comment, may help us to get a fraction closer to a Christian perspective on the conquest of space.

What is man?

Well, as a matter of plainest observation, he is a creature of astounding, prodigious, apparently inexhaustible creative energy.

Which, the believer observes, is exactly what you might hope to find. That is, if he is truly the crowning earthly achievement thus far, of God's ceaseless creativity; since it is perfectly obvious that God is instinct with illimitable, necessarily active creative energy. At this level of understanding and experience, man, God's peculiar handiwork, takes after Father. You would expect him to, on a Christian reckoning.

His problem, from this angle, is finding out what to do with himself; how to expend his energy so as to extend, not confound, his creator's design for living.

The problem is exactly the same in the bosom of any family, that microcosm of man-at-large. 'Finding them something to do', especially in the long summer holidays, is the acid test of the skilled parent. Ordinary, healthy children are bursting with energy. They must express it. They must let off steam. They are incurably, irresistibly lively. Repress them, and you often have a

[1] Psalm 8:3–6. RSV.

21

bored, dangerously mischievous creature on your hands. The devil finds work for idle hands to do. A child must continuously find outlets for his energy which intrigue, attract, satisfy, fulfil.

And, of course, the child is father to the man.

Now, to the Christian who takes the doctrine of creation seriously, there is no doubt at all as to what we are seeing, in the cataracts, the veritable Niagaras of energy cascading vigorously, unceasingly, on every hand in the world about us; and most impressively, diversely, dramatically, in human life.

He is witnessing nothing less—in himself he is *expressing* nothing less—than the raw elemental energy of God himself; the constant overspill—though the word is almost clumsy—into this minute speck of creation, of the power that rolls the stars along. It is none other than the evidence of the Holy Spirit, unresting, omnipresent, at work. In all the commonplace, multifarious activity of nature, and of humanity, in the tiniest trivia and the mightiest splendours of the cavalcade of history, the dynamic energy of the Lord and Giver of Life is ceaselessly expended.

Man is in receipt also, however, of a second unique divine and perilous bestowal—freedom. However limited, finite, it is authentic. God's creatures have undoubted ability to transmute the constant surge of energy he wills them to have, into channels good, bad, but perhaps seldom indifferent. *They* decide, basically, how their divinity of power shall be expended. They are not computers programmed by a celestial hand. They decide their own programme. Nowhere more clearly than here do they show how little less they are than God.

The whole history of the race is the record of what man has done with his critical endowments. He has used them splendidly—and squalidly. He spends them freely in organizing, maintaining, improving the society he lives in. He decides, then pours out his energies in splendid profusion in the progressive endeavour to master and harness his habitat. In short, he pro-creates. At his best, he assists, works alongside his Creator in the progressive completion of what without arrogance we think we recognize, looking about our world, as an extraordinary, engrossing piece of unfinished creative business. And inasmuch as any of his millionfold endeavours make for the enlargement, the joy and splendour of life aboard this planet, he fulfils the design of his Creator; who willed man, and still does will him, 'to put all things under his feet'.

But, alas, this isn't at all the complete picture. How well we know it!

Man hasn't only found splendidly constructive ways to express his power and freedom. He has found it fatally easy to decide to destroy, as well as determine to build. In one sense, he simply hasn't been able to find enough absorption for his torrential energies in the pursuit of joyous fulfilment. Energy and aggression are close neighbours. Times without number, in public and private, man has concluded an unholy alliance between them; fusing the two together to make fearful havoc of his nobler hopes and aspirations.

On his bustling career, the energies of man have found sombre satisfaction and release in immense, furious concentration on the complex, challenging devilry, the fatal fascination of military conquest. The field of human conflict has been far and away the largest acreage, soaked in blood and tears, on which his powers have been tragically dissipated; so wrecking the purpose of the Creator; degrading man not so much to animal as to demonic stature.

Our own day, however, is different. The situation has suddenly, radically changed.

Thermo-nuclear weapons, and equally, the horrific potential of bio-chemical warfare, have at a stroke altered the whole outlook for mankind. Now, genocide, final, irreversible, is thoroughly practicable. A global conflagration, using these ultimate weapons, and a curtain emblazoned with the legend 'overkill' rings down on the human scene. The world becomes a poisoned charnel house. The human experiment is over; at least on this planet.

Man, slow to change, is pondering hard the sombre writing on the wall. He is becoming aware that he must change his traditional style of life, once for all, or his traditional misuse of the divine endowments he has will really be the death of him.

Which is precisely what some scientists (like Desmond Morris in *The Naked Ape*, for instance) fully expect—admittedly with much justification—to happen. Man, they say, cannot change his spots, any more than the leopard. He will try not to, but sooner or later he is bound to go down. Evolution will be too much for him. He will never be able to overcome his built-in aggression, let alone his other self-destructive tendencies.

Is it quite accidental that at this fateful point in time, the space age dawns?

As a Christian, with a stubborn belief in providence, I do not think so. By the same token, neither do I think that it is insignificant that the word most commonly associated with the space programme, is the word 'conquest'; a thoroughly military, aggressive word.

You will quickly see the point I wish to make.

I believe, as a Christian, that it may well be within what Charles Wesley called the 'wise design' of God, that at this critical moment of destiny for the human race (and so for the purpose of the Creator whose intense concern we children of his obviously are) comes, together with the utmost peril, the possibility at least of outwitting it. And at the same time mankind is given a new, radical opportunity to travel on to a far more glorious—if you like, Godly—stage of the evolutionary journey the Creator intends for him. What is betokened by the Apollo missions, the Mariner probes, and the engrossing designs on Dr. Werner von Braun's drawing board of floating laboratories in orbit, and manned space craft for Mars, may well be, and I believe are, the first glimpses of the providential way in which man may be enabled to wrestle constructively with the problems which have led him so bitterly, abominably to betray himself times without number, on his journey in time.

It is entirely as a Christian, rather than as a well-meaning amateur in the crystal ball-gazing business, that I believe this. It is as a Christian that I see, in the conquest of space, a noble and constructive enterprise which, in time, can take and absorb all the freely vouchsafed energies of men so wantonly poured, for so long, so often, into the art of war. This new conquest will call no less for similar dedication and readiness to sacrifice; yet without any elements of hatred or violence. It will answer the deep clamant need for adventure, and that true glory with which human life at its best is so frequently invested, which ennobles, rather than degrades, those who create and share it. It will offer, but so much more magnificently, the same kind of large exhilaration and intense fascination, in which all can share, which traditionally has been reflected in the fears, the sorrows, the exultations of millions envisaging the varied events of the far off battle-field.

All this, I declare, will be of God. In this, we work and shall work with him.

It is with this perspective in mind that I re-read Paul's visionary words to the Romans, declaring that 'we know that to those who love God . . . everything fits into a pattern for good . . .'

What is happening, what I pray and believe *will* happen, along the way to the stars, could be a far greater instance of Paul's insight than anything so far seen in the panorama of human life.

We can find encouragement already from informed minds with no necessary Christian axe to grind. That most mature and informed writer of science fiction, Ray Bradbury, unhesitatingly sees the kind of possibility emerging that we have been discussing. At last, he says, in the conquest of space, man has found a substitute for war, 'with all its excitement, its glory, and its challenge. Only this time we're up against the real enemy, at last'. I remind you how often, from Jules Verne to H. G. Wells, the visions of science fiction seem to have had an uncanny prescience about them in the light of the 'sixties and seventies'.

Again, one can find lively opposition to the view of those who insist that man is predetermined to write his own death warrant one day in thermo-nuclear, bio-chemical or some other terms. This opposition doesn't come always from Christians who might be accused of wishful thinking. Two scientists—an anthropologist and an anatomist—combined to produce a book, *Naked Ape or Homo Sapiens*?[1] in which they argue strenuously that if it was true that man was simply a naked ape and nothing more, blindly conditioned to do nothing but obey his biological urges, he would have perished long since. The fact is, say these writers, that man has *already* elected to change his style of life, down his brief span of evolutionary life. He is not in the grip of a rigid determinism. He can, must and does alter—however slowly and laboriously. He will do so again.

I am not putting any great weight on such testimony. All I am saying is that such convictions strengthen, rather than undermine, the kind of view which I am inviting you to consider here.

I see nothing at all in Christian faith and insight to deny

[1] John Lewis and Bernard Towers, Garnstone Press, 1969.

26

it. Indeed, I believe it coheres with all we believe about the ways of God with men.

At this time, the space age has only just dawned. It is at the stage transport reached when someone invented the chariot. He would be a bold man who could descry the shape of things to come, even half a century hence. He would be foolish indeed who arrogantly asserted that things, apparently impossible today, will remain so for ever. So many seemingly impenetrable barriers have already been so swiftly smashed, that eager hopefulness would seem a far more sensible posture, than dull scepticism.

We shall see: or rather, I believe our descendants will. At the moment, I wish to declare my increasing certainty: that in this new, splendid, non-violent enterprise, in which significantly, those are most heavily involved who could most easily unleash a global holocaust, we Christians are at liberty to see the unfolding of God's larger, liberating purposes for the creature made by him but little less than himself. We can see reasons for a lively belief that man is not doomed to destroy himself, but is destined for an existence far more splendid and sublime than anything he can so far discern.

Paul sums up, elsewhere in the same chapter from which I quoted a minute ago, the sort of pulse-quickening thoughts which you may well feel were prophetic indeed, in the light of our own day.

'In my opinion,' he remarks, 'whatever we may go through now is less than nothing compared with the magnificent future God has planned for us. The whole creation is on tiptoe to see the wonderful sight of the sons of God coming into their own.'[1]

Armstrong and Aldrin, in the light of centuries to come, may be seen to have been members of an uncommonly important reconnaissance team.

It's in the light of this perspective that Christians may most

[1] Rom. 8:18-19. J. B. Phillips.

27

accurately assess such matters as the space programme budget, and may join issue with those indignantly shaking their heads about the vast cost of (say) the Apollo missions, to date.

The truth of course lies rather more in the realm of vision and motive than comparisons; as the critics found, you remember, who muttered furiously in the presence of Jesus about the disgusting waste of money represented by the flask of ointment poured prodigally over him by the woman with a heart of love.

They received their come uppance briskly at his hands. He called their bluff and exposed their humbug. They were eager to be extraordinarily generous—with someone else's money. It wasn't a case of either/or. It seldom is, where money is concerned. Their concern wasn't with the poor. It lay elsewhere—and involved far less reputable emotions.

If what I have said already is anywhere near the truth, the actual cost of the space programme is infinitesimal. It is an overwhelmingly splendid investment; far more so, one might be tempted to argue, than the annual expenditure of the American people on say two luxury items alone—pleasure boats and ski equipment—the yearly bill for which, the *Observer* informed us, would amply cover the NASA annual budget. Such down to earth data help one to get the matter into perspective.

There were probably people around when Cologne cathedral was built who complained bitterly that the time, effort and materials could have built a good many no doubt badly needed peasant dwellings. If so, I expect most of us are glad all the same, that their voices did not prevail. Then, as now, 'either/or' is frequently a shallow antithesis. It certainly is so far as the conquest of space contrasted with (say) the conquest of world poverty is concerned.

All I have tried to say so far reflects what modern Christians have thought for long, about so many of the enterprises of science.

28

What is man? we asked with the Psalmist.

To which, looking at the vast array of men and women dedicating their lives to a hundred different scientific disciplines, day by day, Christians must say: man is a co-worker with God, seeking to unravel the mysteries of the universe; seeking reverently to enlarge his understanding, increase his knowledge, penetrate to the core of reality, embedded in God's creation all around him.

We give the answer more readily, assuredly, joyously, when we think of those, say, who patiently seek to isolate in order to destroy, the rogue element in genetics which produces a mongol child; or to root out the causes of leukaemia, cancer, or insanity. When scientists discover the answer to leprosy, tuberculosis, smallpox, we offer thanks and cry 'What God hath wrought!' and recognize without a moment's hesitation his hand in that of the research chemist and those associated with him.

But we're rather more reluctant to see the same hand at work say in the astounding invention and refinement of computers, or radio communications, or nuclear reactors.

If this sermon can persuade you to take a far more discerning look at the larger face of science and technology, and discover that in and through all science devoted to the enlargement and ennobling of life, we veritably work with God, I shall be happy indeed. For that is the truth of the matter.

After all, what is the raw material of science? Why, nothing less, nothing other than the handiwork of the Creator. So that, in his work, a scientist who is a believer can truly say, with a famous scientist of old, that at his best, he is trying to think God's thoughts after him. He is not laying impious hands on the holy of holies. He is unveiling the truth about God. He is lending a vital hand, in eager communion and co-partnership with the Creator, to complete what is obviously his unfinished creation.

To what end? Why, that in this work, he might glorify

God and enjoy him forever, to quote the old confession; finding in his task an experience in which adoration, activity, strenuous effort, insight, adventure and the rich fulfilment of achievement and creativity are all wondrously blended.

This is not religious romanticism. This is religious realism. It is entirely at one with the Bible view of creation. There, you will find no false infantile division between 'sacred' and 'secular'; but only the final cleavage allowable in Christian thinking, between good and evil; reverence and blasphemy; co-partnership with God, and sinful rebellion against him.

It is now more vital than ever that we lay Christians should see, at his best, the scientist as a co-worker with the Creator, handling with confidence and power the stuff of life; drawing ever nearer, with every move forward which enlarges his understanding and insight, to the skirts of God himself.

Werner von Braun himself, the father of the Saturn rocket, put his finger on the pulse of truth when, thinking no doubt of the Apollo mission and the many more yet to come, he said, 'Through a closer look at creation, we ought to gain a better knowledge of the Creator'. Indeed we should. This is precisely the attitude of the Christian at work in every realm of scientific endeavour.

All of which helps to explain the understandable fact that the scientist at his best often displays the very qualities which Christians recognize as belonging to Godliness; to the work of the Holy Spirit.

Let me read you some splendid words of a Christian who is also an eminent scientist, Professor Charles Coulson. They inspired me years ago on my own quest for understanding, as a layman in this realm. They still express the sublime truth of this matter and sum up far better than any words of mine could hope to do, the insight for which I plead. They are all the more important since they carry the authority of a dedicated scientist.

Think for a moment of some of the attitudes of mind with which any scientist must come to his search; there is honesty, and integrity, and hope; there is enthusiasm, for no one ever yet began an experiment without an element of passion; there is an identification of himself with his experiment . . . there is a humility before a created order of things . . . there is a singleness of mind about the search which reveals what the scientist himself may often hesitate to confess, that he does what he does because it seems exciting and it somehow fulfils a deep part of his very being; there is co-operation with his fellows, both in the same laboratory and across the seven seas; there is patience, akin to that which kept Madame Curie at her self-imposed task of purifying eight tons of pitchblende to extract a few milligrams of radium; above all there is judgement—judgement as to what constitutes reliable research; judgement as to what is fit for publication . . .

And later on he adds:

science (is) one part of religion and *the splendour, the power, the dynamic and progressive character of science are nothing but the splendour and the power and the dynamic character of God, progressively revealed to us. We do them justice as we honour Him.*[1]

And yet . . . there is something else to be said.

More than once, I have used the phrase 'at his best' . . . 'the scientist . . . at his best'. I have qualified what has been said about man the scientist as co-worker with God. You have caught, without doubt, the implications.

What is man?

He is a son of God, to be sure, little less than his Father and, accordingly, sorely tempted to usurp his Father's place. He needs finally to discover the truth of that glorious Christian paradox

[1] *Science and Christian Belief*, Fontana, 1959, pp. 72 f., 82. My italics.

Be my Lord, and I shall be
Firmly bound, for ever free

if he is not to betray himself and his world. Unless he recognizes himself as working with his Father, for his Father's ends, he is sadly likely to make the running for himself, opt for a fading crown, urged on by a fatal itch for power, the roar of the crowd, or the sweetest siren song. He is sadly likely to find (as he has found on innumerable occasions past) his most splendid hopes and aspirations lying in ruins about him.

The way to the stars might yet be fouled. The Saturn rocket on its pad might yet begin to take on the shape of a new-style mobile Tower of Babel, contrived by men who simply want to make a name for themselves, instead of their Maker. The end might still be confusion; with the inter-stellar blueprints and all they might nobly betoken, buried under the rubble. Looking backward to recall not only his triumphs but also the tragedies of man-in-the-making, is still a highly salutary exercise.

Look back now, for a moment.

Do you remember the dramatic symbol of what I am saying, offered to us in the events of 1961? I wrote a piece at the time about it: and entitled it 'Two Men in Boxes'. I wonder if you recall them?

Both boxes were brilliantly designed. One was largely metal, and in it a human being was hurled into space for the first time, there to orbit the earth, and—miracle of miracles—brought safely back to earth again. How remote it seems, now! What a truly epoch-making event it really was! Man dipped his foot into the ocean of outer space, and found the temperature bearable. He exulted in his triumph; as he had a right to do.

The other box, too, was fool-proof; more accurately, bullet-proof. It was made of toughened glass. It was in fact the dock in which, as Gagarin hurtled round the earth, an insignificant, ageing man sat, day by day, in a high court, in Jerusalem. He gazed through the transparent walls at a stony-faced world; of foes understandably implacable. They gazed back at him; and wondered maybe how such a pitiful creature could in fact have been such an appalling monster in the dreadful years gone by.

You remember, of course, though so much has happened since then. The man was Eichmann. His technological achievement had been to hurl skilfully six million tormented Jews into their graves; a triumph of social and scientific engineering. It was a crime of such sickening magnitude, devilry and horror as makes the stomach heave to re-envisage it even today.

The contrast was and is complete. The symbol was unmistakable. There is no need to expound it overmuch.

I have ventured to say today that Gagarin, and those who have flown after him thus far, could be, and in the providence of God are, intended to represent a way in total contrast to the awful hell of outer darkness, self-will and pride, symbolized in that grotesque little man in the Israeli Assize: the hell to which the arrogance and pride which are the true sign of Godlessness, could still consign us.

It need not be. I believe it will not be. I cherish the confidence that God intends us to see in the pioneers of the space age, a vastly different way of responsible, bold and sublime adventure. I believe the way to the stars is intended for mankind as a novel path of redemptive fulfilment.

'Which will you have?' The question arches now, as always, over our civilization. The new cosmic back-drop throws it into fresh relief for us. We shall make reply, one way or the other.

A short parable from Plato's *Republic* seems to speak an apt word to men on the threshold of this new, brilliant, and, as I believe, God-ordained astral pilgrimage. It

33

concerns a shipload of mariners highly dubious about the trustworthiness of their pilot. Night by night he charted his course carefully from the heavens. The man's mad to be stargazing, said the hardheaded sailors. It's plain common sense that the set of the sails, the strength of the wind, the swing of the tiller, determine the safety of the ship. He'll have us in trouble. Away with him! So, wise fellows, they clapped the pilot in the hold. They battened the hatches down on him. They sailed on blithely keeping their eyes away from the sky.

And the ship was wrecked.

Do you recall that final New Testament word from Jesus, as imagined by John, the sage and seer?

'I, Jesus, have sent my angel to you with this testimony for the churches. I am the root and scion of David, the bright morning star.'[1]

The bright morning star . . . in its unchanging, immovable and eternal splendour, akin to what Shakespeare says about love, in his immortal sonnet. Love, which is

> *the ever-fixed mark*
> *That looks on tempests, and is never shaken . . .*

It is a cliché these days to talk about the shaking of the foundations, under the impact of the winds of change now howling at cyclone force. It is equally, gloriously true to declare as Christians may yet do, that Jesus, the bright morning star of hope and truth, shines immovable in majesty and truth, in our enlarging sky. We believe with increasing joy and certainty that Isaac Watts' familiar lines still hold nothing but the truth.

> *Jesus shall reign where'er the sun*
> *Doth his successive journeys run;*
> *His kingdom stretch from shore to shore,*
> *Till suns shall rise and set no more.*

He still announces his identity, to those who will keep company with him, seeing in him the embodiment of the

[1] Rev. 22:16.

34

eternal Creator; the mediator, declaring the ways of God to men; and the true, eternal fulfilment, on earth or in the heavens, of man; made but little less than his Creator. Christ remains the ever-fixed Lord of all; the healer of pride and vainglory; the one who reconciles man to his proper role as a son of the Father whose glory fills the skies; the Father whose desire begins to shine ever more clearly for his sons to come into their own, as they begin to invade and subdue more fully, his boundless dominion in space, as well as time.

We who glory in our inheritance in Christ are assured now as never before, that the heavens are telling the glory of God; that his steadfast love extends to them. We are exalted to think that even though men may take the wings of the morning and dwell in the deepest ocean of space, even there shall the hand of God lead them, and his right hand shall cover them; to bless them still with all his fulness, who is in all, and through all, and over all.

Blessed be the God and Father of our Lord Jesus Christ! By this great mercy we have been born anew to this living hope!

3) Are You a Neophiliac?

THERE are some snatches of the Old Testament and New which earn instant recognition. You don't have to pause to identify them.

Here is one. You would have known where it came from, even if we hadn't read the story—one of the best known in the world's literature—a few minutes ago.

And when he came to himself . . .

When he came to his senses . . . thus the New English Bible—a lively alternative, and no quarrel with it. But somehow, for once, the Authorised Version has the edge on the NEB in the matter of crystal clarity. When the moment of truth came, the man concerned was really beginning again to come not only to his senses . . . but also to himself.

And when he came to himself . . . there began what we'll call, please, the last stage of a five-act drama. I put it that way for a particular reason. This week, I read a large and fascinating tract for the times with mounting interest and indeed real excitement—and, finally, to my comfort, as a Christian—using that grand word in its strict sense, *cum-forte*, 'with strength'. It prompted me immediately to re-read that poignant, indelible story of a stupid boy and his loving father. If you yourself have read the recent book to which I refer, you will have no difficulty in identifying it as I describe the story of the prodigal son as a five act drama in which initial anticipation led direct to a dream, which, in turn, heralded growing frustration. At last, the dream dissolved horridly into a nightmare, preceding what might have been an explosion into final disaster, but which, instead, had a gloriously happy ending.

A brief recap of the story, then, in these terms.

The first act we may call the Anticipation Stage. It began at home, against the intolerably tame backdrop of humdrum life on the farm. Long hours, hard work, little play, less fun. It was ordered, secure—and altogether dull. His ego reared up in strong rebellion against the dead monotony of it all: the stuffy paternalism, the needling dependence. He began to dream . . . of what life was like where the action was—in the city, where a man might find colourful deliverance from this pointless drudgery.

'Father, give me!' He wanted it now. His share of the property. The means to get up and go—without waiting. The property wasn't his. But his father, with veiled dismay and enormous discretion, let the lad have his way. What use would it have been to play the heavy-handed parent, to have kept his son under his thumb, eating his heart out in sullen growing resentment?

So, anticipation passed from thought to action. Act two, the Dream Stage; with money to burn, no restrictions, and the heady delights of city life, anonymous, free from the damning respectability of home and family. It was just as he had imagined it. Thrills, gaiety; wine, women and song; and the day in which to sleep. The dream flowed on; hypnotic, compulsive; splendidly successful, satisfying . . . live now, pay later . . .

Only it wasn't quite like that. 'Pay later' wasn't possible. It was cash on the nail—and resources steadily dwindled. The third act dawned; the Frustration Stage. Coming events cast uneasy shadows before them. The prodigal clung on, Micawber like, waiting for something to turn up. No risk, no return, Surely, if he laid out his money, cultivated the acquaintance of the smart set, he would be bound to make the right contacts to ensure his survival when the money ran out? All the same, the mornings after the night before grew more and more frightening. Hangovers wouldn't lift. Depression clamped down. The day of reckoning came to meet him at fearful speed.

Finally, it arrived—the fourth act of the drama—in which the dream had turned itself inside out. No longer a dream; a nightmare. A nightmare in which the fine clothes and luxury living, disappeared as swiftly as the fine friends, turning to fleece some other victim. A friend in need is a friend indeed. But they don't live in Vanity Fair. 'No-one gave him anything.' Penniless, beaten and broken, he faced the ultimate humiliation: the total wreckage of his pride, and his plans.

An explosion, in a manner of speaking, had taken place. Reality had taken over again. Life had blown up in his face. His dream world had burst into fragments. The only stark, horrid reality was the fact of his empty belly, his forfeited manhood: and the grim awareness of his head-strong lunacy.

So, the final act of the drama might have finished—and does still, in the twentieth century, a thousand times over, when the story is played for real. A fatal overdose, a gas-filled kitchen, a rubber tube from the car exhaust: the traditional quick way out of shame and humiliation, when life—by which I mean reality—has pushed a man up hard and contemptuously against the intolerable reflection of his own failure—an object of derision. He simply can't take it. The death-wish comes upon him. In a torment of despair and isolation, life ends; not with a bang, but a whimper of anguish.

But it didn't happen that way, with the prodigal.

The fifth act arrived, on cue. But it meant an explosion into life, not death. Memory intervened and hope revived. Remorse gripped the hand of resolve. 'I will set off and go to my father', said the son, 'and say to him, "Father, I have sinned, against God and against you; I am no longer fit to be called your son . . .".[1]

The final act of the tragedy was averted. Deliverance, instead of death. Reconciliation superseded ruin. The boy came home to himself, as well as to his rejoicing father. The loving relationship, broken by the barrier of self-centred, self-willed fantasy, was restored. The boy now saw where true fulfilment, true freedom, genuine blessing and joy, was to be found. Salvation came to that household. It began, when the son came to himself. It was made possible only by the father's love.

Now: if your reading happens to have coincided with my own, you will have recognized the sort of language just used to describe the five stages of the brief domestic drama of Luke fifteen.

You will know that the Anticipation, Dream, Frustration, Nightmare, and final Explosion into reality are the headings used in a remarkable book (issued just as the last decade closed) to describe what is called there the 'fantasy cycle' so often and painfully experienced by modern man, and spectacularly indeed over the years of the 'fifties and 'sixties, which have witnessed such a root-and-branch revolution in English social life.

The book is Christopher Booker's *The Neophiliacs*.[2] I focus upon it now since it seems to me a book likelier than most—certainly, far far likelier than say any normal religious paperback by howsoever popular a church leader or theologian—to encourage today's people to look again, with understanding eyes, at the world around them, and, at the same time, to reconsider the claims of the Christian faith to offer modern man a firm vantage point from which to try to make liberating sense of the tumultuous world in which he lives.

[1] Luke 15:17–18.
[2] Collins, 1969.

It is not I believe accidental that of the twenty or so people I have spoken to recently about this book, those who had read it were keen young university types; one and all impressed by its argument.

It is written by one of the highly talented trendsetters of the last decade: a leading representative, indeed, of that generation of colourful people from Oxbridge and (equally) elsewhere, who have made an indelible mark upon our life and bewildering, dizzying radical times; the times indeed of the neophiliac—the novelty-addict, forever chasing the latest sensation.

Booker's name regularly rolled across your television screen a few years ago, as a resident script writer for the programme which perhaps more than anything else was the symbol of the shrill winds of social change, *That Was the Week That Was*. He was also one of the original editing team of *Private Eye*: not that one would expect even this lively church congregation to belong by and large to its dedicated readership!

Now this is (I hope) a sermon, not an audible book review. Bear with me, however, as I try to summarize the main idea *The Neophiliacs* so compulsively expounds. It is all of a piece with Luke fifteen.

With brilliant skill the author achieves the almost impossible task of describing, then interpreting, what he rightly calls the revolution in English life during the 'fifties and 'sixties; dynamic, devastating decades during which it has seemed at times nothing could escape de-bunking, doubt, demolition or all three—from the political establishment to sexual morality, from modes and manners to the entire structure and tradition of the Christian faith. At the same time, an astounding technological revolution was and still is rocketing along, breathlessly hurrying us into new affluence as well as attitudes and patterns of life. From the first man on the moon to heart transplants, from the Cuba Crisis to the Six Day War, from 'God is dead' to 'Oh, Calcutta', from Congo to Vietnam, from the drug scene to the demo., from protest to all embracing permissiveness, from legal abortions to legal homosexuality and the Pill, the Moors murders to the Great Train Robbery, Powellism to the battle of Grosvenor Square, the Kennedys to Martin Luther King, ear and eye, heart and mind, have been assailed and assaulted continuously down these years with sights and sounds, ideas and events, variously awesome or appalling, but almost always deeply challenging. These have been the triumphant decades of technocrat, admass, automation and instant everything—especially communication, via the ubiquitous Pandora's box with the glass screen in everybody's corner. In some senses they have been indeed the years the adman has eaten; ministering to our every novel appetite and fancy, however crazy or perverted.

Vogue has been all; seen continuously in the harsh glare of huge bonfires fired by volatile candour, on which inhibitions and restraints have been unceremoniously burnt up; years when the mightily respectable have been cast down from their thrones, even if the meek have yet to inherit the earth.

Is there any key to an understanding of our times? Is there a 'common thread' binding together the so wildly contrasting strands in the gaudy pattern of our society, in which, often, disenchantment, disgust, destruction and despair have proved the pay-off to so much eager experiment, so many high hopes, so much revolutionary change? For no period, says Booker, has exposed the sheer hollowness of the libertarian and technological dreamfantasies of the twentieth century so much as the last twenty years. Man's thrusting efforts to rid himself of his traditional taboos, and bend his environment totally to his will, have not only seen the erection of splendid cities, super highways, modern schools and hospitals, health and welfare services. They have also seen the emergence of new, strange, daunting evils—of unparalleled noise and squalor; the relentless pollution of the environment and the hideous wholesale slaughter of humankind and wildlife alike: both careless and calculating. They have been years of growing tension, alienation, isolation, frustration; discord and disruption, private insecurity, shattered belief and aspirations: all producing in turn the kind of psychic epidemics to which C. G. Jung refers when, in his *Modern Man in Search of a Soul*,[1] he says:

It is becoming more and more obvious that it is not starvation, not microbes, not cancer, but man himself who is mankind's greatest danger, because he has no adequate protection against psychic epidemics, which are infinitely more devastating in their effect than the greatest natural calamities.

The last twenty years have seen plenty, contributing both as cause and effect to the inevitably neurotic attitude to life of those to whom Martin Esslin referred in his so significantly entitled Penguin, *Absurd Drama*. He says:

For many intelligent human beings, the world of the mid-twentieth century has lost its meaning and has simply ceased to make sense. Previously held certainties have dissolved, the firmest grounds for hope and optimism have collapsed. Suddenly man sees himself faced with a universe that is both frightening and illogical—in a word, absurd. All assurances of hope, all explanations of ultimate meaning have suddenly been unmasked as nonsensical illusions, empty chatter, whistling in the wind.

Such sombre assessments could be duplicated and reduplicated a hundred times from thoughtful observers of the modern scene.

Now: back to the question. Is there any key to an understanding of these years?

[1] Routledge, 1933.

42

Indeed there is, says Christopher Booker.

It is found in man's immemorial tendency to run away from reality, at the bidding of an insatiable urge for self-assertion—an urge which leads him recklessly to abandon or indeed destroy the law-and-order pattern of life into which he enters: the established order, the *status quo*. Seized of an overwhelming urge to satisfy his itch for novelty, power, pleasure, sensation, adulation, he constructs a world not of reality, but fantasy, built on the shifting sands of his own aggressive, shortsighted self-centredness. Out of it, the whole tragedy of the human dilemma emerges, so brilliantly discerned by the great dramatists—from the Greek tragedians to Shakespeare. What are Mark Antony, Macbeth, Othello, if not spinners of splendid fantasies leading to their own downfall and disaster?

Men in every age (and spectacularly our own, in which so much seems larger than life) set out blindly, with immense determination, to bend the world around them to ends dictated by their own pride and self-sufficiency. They seek fulfilment in a dream world ministering to their own natural instinct for self-aggrandisement. Man sets in motion a fantasy cycle through which, inexorably, he comes to grief and brings others down with him.

During the dream stage all goes well. But the frustrations inherent in any pattern of life founded upon falsehood and disunity must soon show themselves. The dream dissolves into nightmare. Man fashions a world not of God's design, but his own disorder; a prodigal society. The day of reckoning arrives. Life disintegrates, as it always must, unless one's way of life is founded, not upon rebellion against ultimate truth, but co-operation with and obedience to that truth.

Interestingly, Booker nowhere mentions the parable of the prodigal son. But reading *The Neophiliacs*, one is struck again and again by the way in which in fact Jesus' immortal story illumines the history of our frenzied decades, at once showing inextricably mingled the signs both of grandeur and of *folie de grandeur*, of splendour and squalor.

This tale is timeless. It is not simply a parish pump incident of domestic stress and strain. It is a token-story, a model of mankind. It speaks to our condition and exposes it. Best of all, it points the way to our release and relief, our deliverance and our salvation.

Look again at more of the evidence—so plentiful, so contrasting—of this over-arching fact of life.

Some time ago the *Observer* published a series of articles under the intriguing title 'The Sad Society'.

Week by week, it offered arresting profiles of a number of sad citizens.

Destitute? Social misfits? People on whom natural disaster and calamity had fallen? The socially inadequate, the delinquent, modern prodigals, starving and suicidal?

Not in the least.

These were successful men and women from the élite; living in luxury, enjoying incomes and amenities way beyond the average. They had worked hard, struck it rich. Or fortune had simply smiled on them.

And, astonishingly, they were one and all basically sad. They had achieved it seemed everything but happiness. *Joie de vivre* had eluded them. Their mode and manner of life, for all their comfort and power, was gloomy, not gay. None of them had achieved permanent satisfying relationships, loving and loved. They were emotionally brittle, edgy, disenchanted.

What had gone wrong?

It would be easy—and stupid—to over-simplify. Yet it would still be fair to say that if these were lost souls, it was because, by and large, they had forgotten, if ever they had known, that man does not live by spin driers and colour television alone, not by swanning round the globe

44

by jet, but by every word of peace and power, truth and goodness, spoken deep in his hungry heart, by the living God.

There was no indication, so far as one could tell, that any of these highly fortunate, sadly run-down characters had grasped that life, at its best, and practically speaking, was essentially a matter of giving rather than receiving; and that life lived in simple obedience to the threefold fantasy-imperative 'I see: I want: I take' could only lead in the long run to disenchantment and disgust.

These lives, too, had exploded into reality—over the years. They were prodigals whose money had not dried up, but whose life had withered all the same. Their private dreams realized, they had found themselves empty still; basically distressed; fed up and far from home.

The title of the series seemed to suggest they were far from being odd exceptions to the rule.

Take another aspect of the fantasy cycle—the life and distressful times of young John Bull, drug addict: or his sad sister Jane.

It may indeed have been John's social inadequacy or his poor background which eased him first on to the slippery slope. On the other hand, we have all heard and read over these frantic years, of John the undergraduate with the world at his feet, and Jane, from a stable suburban middle class home surrounded from birth with affection and security. Their name, alas, if not legion, is well-known.

How did John start out on his journey to the far country?

To be sure, not at all through any spectacular wickedness. He simply wanted to be footloose and fancy free. He was exhibiting what Booker—along with orthodox Christians down the centuries—calls the 'fatal flaw' at the heart of human nature—a flaw rooted in the self, unrelated to any consideration other than personal satisfaction.

45

John began dabbling in drugs for one simple reason: to please himself. It was just an act of self-assertion. No thought of the possible pain he might inflict on others, or on society, entered his head, or, if it did, he dismissed it. His itch for compensation or sensation (other words for self-satisfaction) was the dominant factor. It was his undoing.

It was a fascinating escape route. It led him out of the world of reality. He blundered step by step across its frontiers into the fantasy world of so-called expanded consciousness, heightened sensitivity—a seductive, exciting world, but totally unreal. The bleak or deadly tedium of everyday life was left behind, if only for the time being. A new heady delight was savoured. The hunger for it grew, silently, strongly.

Anticipation had moved to the dream stage. All went well. But the appetite still grew by what it fed on. Much wanted more—and then yet more. To get the kicks which had produced such transports in the early days, you needed more and more fuel for the fire. It now blazed furiously: its flames leapt higher. Drugs cost money. Money must therefore be acquired . . . somehow . . . anyhow. Sometimes, the dream violently wrenched itself into a nightmare, and the deadly explosion into reality rushed upon the victim with shattering speed: as in the case of the erstwhile happy schoolboy of fourteen from a very normal home, on a Bank Holiday spree at the seaside, who, high on a lethal mixture of pep pills and beer, gaily ran into the ocean fully clothed and drowned himself.

He was exceptional, of course. The more exquisite suffering was reserved, and still is, for less dramatic characters—run of the mill long-term drug takers, whose abject dependence on larger and still larger supplies meant, and still does mean, in practical terms a constant nightmare and misery, degradation, anxiety and despair . . . for which 'hell' would be an apt description. John and Jane, held in the grip of a bondage far more terrible than anything they knew in the old innocent days of tame boredom and teenage frustration, know that freak-out, comedown, and the unspeakable craving for yet another trip, together make up a world in which joy and reality have together taken flight. They are in a far country of terror and tragedy: and they know what has already happened to the others.

Of course, they might just conceivably have been warned off: any alcoholic, any nicotine addict coughing his life away, poor wretch, in a lung cancer ward could have told John or Jane what they might be in for. But the fatal fantasy flaw in human nature won't permit the victim to learn. He knows already—until reality mocks him—and he discovers his ignorance and abysmal folly too late . . .

Nothing in this sad tragic tale of sophisticated fantasy is more symbolic than the experience of those six Pennsylvania students who, freaked out in a meadow one brilliant summer afternoon, woke up from their drugged sleep two hours later to discover that, as they had sunbathed, their open eyes had been gazing, unconsciously, into the direct glare of the strong sunshine. They woke up blind; their sight permanently destroyed. They have the rest of their lives to reflect, in darkness, on the true meaning of what seemed harmless, thrilling fantasy.

Wherever you look, life mirrors the selfsame picture.

Raise the hallowed battlecry 'Freedom!' for instance. Reject mockingly the eternal truth that sex, on the one hand, and on the other love, companionship, tenderness and loyalty must forever be conjoined and only parted at risk. Deride the traditional sanctions of sexual restraint and discipline as false and anti-human. Go in for fantasy.

47

Erect sex as a satisfying goal in itself. Exploit the urge in massive, sophisticated fashion. Then sit back and observe what happens, in terms of dream turned nightmare—the 1,200 young British school girls around twelve to fourteen aborted last year (only a few years ago, a sixth of that figure); a new and daunting VD epidemic; a coarsening, not an enrichment, of human life in general: a diminution of joy, overall, a sad bondage of the human spirit—not its liberation.

Look at the haunting spectres from farther afield: Jew and Arab baring their teeth and brandishing their automatic weapons: each in his own way the victim, like larger but often no more enlightened neighbours, of the huge fantasy of nationalism. Or consider the uneasy South African aware that his apartheid dream is dissolving into a nightmare: that his lovely country is a smouldering volcano of bitterest hatred, threat and menace . . . the fantasy-cycle revolving inexorably . . .

Now: in emphasizing at length this dreadful side of the human story, I am neither attempting to work up a fine head of steaming moral indignation, nor seeking a vantage point from which to play the Blame Game. I am simply saying again, as a modern Christian, that when men backtrack from God, the source of life, sanity, and wisdom; the great Author and Original of goodness and truth—then they increase their peril with every step they take, further and further into the never-never land of fantasy, in which anything is possible—indeed, probable—except health, joy, peace, for mind and heart.

It was particularly interesting—almost startling—to find that the author of *The Neophiliacs* apparently emphasizes the same conclusion in the final section of his book, in which he attempts to grasp the inner meaning of his story of these years.

'Of course,' he remarks, 'what I have been describing as

fantasy or neurosis is what was known to former ages as evil.'[1]

Well, a rose by any other name . . . call it evil, call it a fatal flaw, call it schizophrenia or fantasy, one thing is clear. Man needs deliverance from it.

But *how*?

Here, *The Neophiliacs* stops short. The author cannot offer much more than earnest exhortation. He says:

Ultimately to overcome his own fantasy-self is the one supreme contribution that a man can make to mankind. All the fantasies that are around us, that infect the collective human organism, are in the end just one fantasy, made up of all the separate unresolved images and acts of self-assertion that are fed into it from each individual fantasy-self of all the thousands of millions of human beings on earth. Every man who asserts his own ego against the general framework in any way, however small . . . is playing his tiny part in increasing the sum of the world's discords and miseries . . . However much one wishes to change the outside world, the only thing one can change or have any control over is ultimately oneself. Which is why the greatest good any man can do to change the world is the least dramatic act of all—to withdraw his own contribution from the general sum of evil.[2]

And he quotes approvingly an old Vietnamese who, when the Vietnam war was at its height, and his country was being so cruelly torn to pieces around him, simply said:

Humanity is *one*. Each of us is responsible for his personal actions, and his actions towards the rest of

[1] p. 308.
[2] p. 330.

humanity. All we can do is to hold back our own brand from the fire. Pull it back—do not add to the flame.

He adds a word likewise from Carl Jung:

> . . . a man knows that whatever is wrong in the world is in himself, and if he only learns to deal with his own shadow, then he has done something real for the world. He has succeeded in removing an infinitesimal part at least of the unsolved, gigantic social problems of our day.

Amen!

But what is there here that men have not known all along?

The heart of the problem still remains.

How do you reach out to put a new heart into man, so that he no longer *wishes* to head for the far country? So that he recognizes the difference between fantasy and reality; and *wants* to deal, and *learns* to deal, with 'what is wrong in himself'; to hold back his own brand from the fire of the world's ills and evil.

'The good which I want to do, I fail to do,' cried a sensitive soul, centuries ago. 'But what I do is the wrong which is against my will . . . I discover this principle, then: that when I want to do the right, only the wrong is within my reach. In my inmost self I delight in the law of God, but I perceive that there is in my bodily members a different law, fighting against the law that my reason approves and making me a prisoner . . . Miserable creature that I am, who is there to rescue me out of this body doomed to death?"[1]

You remember that heart cry. It came from Paul, that representative man, confessing the daemonic power which had wrecked and ruined his good intentions; which had thrust him forward, remorselessly, along a prodigal track of life he knew perfectly well sense and wisdom should

[1] Romans 7:19–24.

lead him to avoid. But his was not just a cry of despair and defeat from the fantasy world of rebellion against the good. He answers his own question, with glorious confidence, joy, and total conviction. He had been made a new man, a new creature; old things had passed away; all things had become new.

'Who is there to rescue me . . .?' he cries. 'God alone, through Jesus Christ our Lord! Thanks be to God!'[1]

Once, says my Gospel, there stepped upon the arena of history a man like all men, yet raised—and here is the splendid, but by no means blind or irrational mystery of the Incarnation—to unheard of heights of moral and spiritual grandeur. No demi-god, no pseudo-human, his life was open to the closest scrutiny. Men saw that the vital, unique fact of his appearing (and Christians have believed it ever since) was that he was in such communion from first to last with God, the Father and Redeemer— communion unbroken by sin and self—that what in others betrayed them ever and anon into playing the prodigal, was in him harmonized and woven into an unflawed pattern of life.

Because he was a man, he was in all points tempted like as we are, which meant his own peculiarly subtle temptations—as Christopher Booker himself shrewdly sees in a remarkable passage—to contrive a fantasy world of his own, by abusing, rather than using—even in the very highest interests—the giant powers of mind and spirit with which he knew himself invested.

One step out of the path of total unswerving obedience to the full-orbed truth and will of the Father, and he would have joined, at however exalted a level, the common ruck of prodigals.

We can only stand afar off and wonder with awe at the

[2] Romans 7:25.

unimaginable strength of the impulses beckoning him away from the path of total obedience.

'You are the Son of God!' whispered the tempter. 'You have been baptised with the Holy Spirit. You know your mission is to proclaim the Kingdom. You are equipped for the task. But here you are—forty days without food, in this wilderness! Prove to yourself that God is with you! Tell these stones to become bread!'

And Jesus stood poised, as he did later on the parapet of the temple, to exploit God's gift, instead of laying it on the altar of a perfect self-sacrifice; to reassure himself— which would have been an act of unfaith—to compel faith, rather than win it, which in the very process would have crumbled into a strengthless counterfeit. He stood poised, that is to say, on the brink of his own unique fantasy—the expression of self-assertion, however exalted, however noble. The alternative was a continuing total surrender to God. To swerve would have been but slightly removed from reality, at that stage. But it would have been of self-will, not of God; belonging to the Kingdom of darkness rather than light.

'*Once again the devil took him to a very high mountain, and showed him all the kingdoms of the world in their glory. "All these", he said, "I will give you, if you will only fall down and do me homage." But Jesus said, "Begone, Satan! Scripture says, 'You shall do homage to the Lord your God and worship him alone.'"*'

'*Then the devil left him; and angels appeared and waited on him . . .*'[1]

Here is the language of myth and symbol, of course. Scholars and saints have sought in every age to plumb its meaning. To me, it speaks of Jesus' own victorious encounter with the temptation to enter a fantasy world in which self-will would have dictated short cuts to bend men's minds and lever their loyalties, instead of seeking

[1] Matt. 4:8–11.

at infinite cost, to win their free response to the call of God; the inner summons of goodness and truth.

Instead, again and again, men discovered that undeniable summons in his words and works of entreaty, appeal, self-evident moral authority. Thus he became to them, both the true and living Way, and also the living inspiration kindling new, holy desires to own him as Lord and discover his secret for themselves. They found themselves, in his presence, drawn to cherish no longer the fantasy world of self and pride, splintering and fracturing relationships, but reborn, living in a new world—the world of the Kingdom—the Kingdom of God; the world of joyous, substantial reality; of mercy, love, self-forgetfulness, grace and forgiveness; an invisible yet indestructible world.

Men found in his presence they tended to lose both inclination and capacity for evil, rebellion, fantasy. They found themselves stretching out to achieve something strangely akin, and yet splendidly different; beholding not fantasy but vision. The vision of God: and God's world, renewed by goodness and love. The beatific vision which has haunted men down the long centuries, to their great and endless comfort.

'*I am the light of the world,*' *said the Lord of life.* '*No follower of mine shall wander in the dark; he shall have the light of life*' . . . '*If you dwell within the revelation I have brought, you are indeed my disciples; you shall know the truth, and the truth shall set you free*'. . . '*If then the Son sets you free, you will indeed be free*' . . .[1]

Free, that is, of the dust—the glitter-powder of vanity and self-deception—which life so easily flings into the eyes of self-willed men, to their dire confusion and distress

'*What do you want me to do for you?*' asks the Lord of life of a poor sufferer by the roadside.

'*Master!*' cries the victim, '*I want my sight back.*'

[1] John 8:12, 31–36.

Man still stands there, for all his astounding achievements in art and science, hapless and helpless, along the modern tarmac. The Christ who is the same yesterday, today and for ever, also stands there, regnant and timeless the Saviour of men, able to enlighten the eyes of everyman's mind and spirit; to reclaim the prodigal, to lift him from the nightmare of darkness and defeat into which his self-will has betrayed him.

Said Luther, quaintly, centuries ago—'In order to experience sun and joy, it is indeed impossible to conjure it up as by magic in your heart; you must jump out of the dark house of your life into the sun.'

It is that jump—the leap of faith, powered by strong, sober reason and reflection finally spurred by the intolerable awareness that you are a prodigal, bedraggled and spent, but born for victory and defeat—it is that jump of faith, which brings healing, deliverance, light and joy.

'*Go,*' said Jesus to the blind man; '*your faith has cured you.*' *And at once he recovered his sight and followed him on the road.*[1]

It is the road to reality, still.

> *Be Thou my Vision, O Lord of my heart;*
> *Naught be all else to me, save that Thou art—*
> *Heart of my own heart, whatever befall,*
> *Still be my Vision, O Ruler of all!*

[1] Mark 10:51–52.

4) A Matter of Motives

THE other Saturday morning, I found myself standing on a corner of the High Street, conscious of a slightly nervous sense of over-exposure clutching my collecting can and the absurd little cardboard tray of paper emblems. It was Princess Elizabeth Day. Like thousands of other helpers, I was all set to win friends and influence people into parting with their loose change (more if possible) on behalf of the thousands of boys and girls cared for in hundreds of Children's Homes up and down the country, staffed by a host of fellow citizens of yours and mine; without whose service and sacrifice Britain would be poor indeed.

A magnificent cause . . . ! The needy, neglected, helpless children . . . ah, but was it really, truly, solely in their interests I stood there a trifle sheepishly, with my tray and tin? I found myself asking the question—and not for the first time. Was compassion my one and only motive? Were there others? Did I half-unconsciously hope to improve the image of the Church? (For I was careful to wear my dog collar—but of course!) Was I secretly hankering after a Little Jack Horner glow? Was I all unconsciously wanting to add fresh lustre to my halo? Was I really trying to outwit and avoid that little stab of conscience which would without doubt have made me miserable, had I left it to my church members, and neglected to take my share of the day's voluntary service?

The questions were pertinent. They posed themselves sharply. I wasn't in a fretful, morbid state of mind. I was carrying out part of the Christian's regular discipline, as

55

I understand it. I was trying to be honest; not in a pernickety way, but with (I trust) a sensible end in view: that self-knowledge which is the beginning of wisdom, and often of grace. I was taking a look at that so often confused and murky sector of the human heart, where motives germinate.

'How happy', exclaimed Jesus on that celebrated hillside occasion, to those who had gathered to hear him, 'how happy are the pure in heart! For they shall see God.'

What did they make of the saying?

Professor William Barclay makes the meaning crystal clear.

'Oh, the bliss of the man whose motives are entirely unmixed, for that man shall see God!'

And elsewhere, he makes clear that by 'entirely unmixed' he means 'absolutely pure'.[1]

Was I absolutely pure in heart, standing there in the bright morning sunshine, wheedling money out of the passers by?

Is absolute purity of heart often or indeed ever found, in this muddy world?

It was that kind of question which led me straight back to the ancient tale, so full of charm, vitality and interest—the story of Elisha and the wealthy woman of Shunem; and, in particular, to the answer she gave to the prophet's question.

'Can I put in a good word for you to the king, or perhaps the army commander?' enquired Elisha. 'Is there anything we can do for you?'

The woman probably shook her head and smiled slightly; then answered the question with firmness but delicacy.

'I live with my own people about me', she said simply. And that was the end of the matter, so far as she was concerned.

[1] *Daily Study Bible*, Matthew Vol. 1. pp. 101–103.

It happened three thousand years ago, give or take a century or two. Elisha was a rugged, austere, prophetic leader, with no credentials save those emerging from his own spiritual stature; who, because of that stature, had the ear of king and commoner alike.

The woman lived near Shunem; married, childless, a lady of property—and personality. It was she who'd pressed Elisha, footslogging it along the hot and dusty road, to turn in for a friendly meal on occasion. It was she who had put it to her compliant husband (how delicately the idea comes over that this lady of determination and kindliness was the executive officer of the household!) that a cool little rest room on the roof of their dwelling, with a bed, a table, a chair and a lamp, might be vastly acceptable to this obvious man of God; and it had been done. Elisha was duly, deeply grateful for such extra-ordinary generosity.

From what motive did it spring, he may have wondered. Perhaps some unacknowledged desire to break out of that small town circle underlay this superbly tactful kindness, this blessed boon of a quiet place of rest for which the weary traveller was so thankful? So Elisha may have thought; asking the woman if there was anything, in turn, they could do for her? A word in the right quarter . . . ?

But no. I live with my own people about me, said the lady with dignity. No, I need nothing. I ask nothing. What has been done, was done out of a desire to help; nothing more; nothing less.

Actually, if you read the rest of the eventful chapter,[1] you find Elisha did discover a most vital service to render her; which led, in the fullness of time, to some domestic high drama. But that's literally another story.

What I'd like to focus upon, as a starting point—slight but significant—is that here was a woman, like quite a few

[1] II Kings 4.

more such women in the Bible record, actually with a single, simple, unmixed motive—a desire to do a little good, for goodness' sake. She was pure in heart; in this matter, at least.

Some people, peering closely at the mainsprings of the human personality, have sometimes concluded that purity of heart, perfectly unselfish action, is to all intents and purposes a flight of fancy; hardly ever a fact.

Take this psychologist's verdict, for instance.

Some people are afraid to face their own characters, and live in unconscious dread of having to admit that their highest motives are second-rate, and their lives selfish and self-seeking. It is usually the 'good' people in this world who suffer most from that terror. In point of fact, pure philanthropy is practically non-existent at our present stage of evolution. We are kind, generous, unselfish, sympathetic and public-spirited largely because it suits us and satisfies our craving for self-approbation to be so.

Agreed? Is there one crumb of comfort you can extract from that blunt analysis?

If so, it is in that word 'largely'. It just leaves a slim chink in the wall of self-interest, through which, from time to time, thank God, you can hope to—and now and again do—see the sheer loveliness of true self-forgetfulness peeping through . . . in the life of everyday people; in the unexpected kindliness of a generous word, a kindly act, a gesture of untainted goodwill; colourful flashes of purity and love, serving to illuminate the grey back-drop of our normal landscape dominated by self-interest and pride.

The tragedy is that such glimpses, such flashes, are so fleeting, frail, infrequent—like the one pure note that a toddler toying with a violin might produce almost by accident, in contrast with the horrible cacophony which he would go on to make, if he continued to experiment.

The Christian faith insists that however incredible it may seem, man, the moral toddler, can grow up in all things, into Christ; to learn, however agonizingly slowly, to make melody in his heart and life—the melody of the God who is love, and life, and liberty; learning the discipline of the Master which can make him truly, habitually, pure in heart, freed from the childish limitations of self and pride; able to achieve that life of love which means purity of heart, and fullness of joy.

But, to begin with, he has to face up to things as they are; to himself as, without Christ, he is.

Self-interest, of course, is not always ugly, objectionable, abhorrent. It can wear an eminently respectable face. It can look, and indeed to an extent actually be, admirable; deserving of respect and applause. Singleminded determination to succeed, for instance, is an extremely common disguise in which self-interest garbs itself. Who would want to quarrel with it?

Listen to this for example; an honest testimony, from an honest man; a picturesque personality in the House of Commons; everybody knows him, and certainly nobody can ignore him! He is under no illusions about the relentless, surging drive which has whipped him on to make a name for himself on the Westminster scene; a confessedly self-made man, giving us the major clue to his colourful career.

I believe that men are either born with ambition or without it . . . I have been driven remorselessly by ambition all my life; to excel at everything I do, to work harder than the man next door to me, and to climb in my profession. At fifty three years of age, it has not deserted me, and much more remains to be done. I do not lust for power: indeed, I am rather embarrassed by it and the loneliness it brings. I still prefer the 'spit and sawdust' of a public house to the cocktail lounge at the Dorchester. But the driving ambition is there all the time, and it accounts for much that I have done, for good or bad, in my life.[1]

Who is speaking here? That fascinating character, Sir Gerald Nabarro; unapologetic, accurate; spotlighting the compulsive motive—personal ambition—to come out on top, which has thrust him on without respite to make a name, as we said, *for himself:* as all of us want to do, if we're honest. It is a singleminded motive. Is it *pure*, at the same time, in the sense Jesus used the word? In the sense that the heart of the wealthy woman of Shunem was pure?

No, of course not.

Then is it the self-description of a conscienceless rogue, a deplorable villain?

To suggest such a thing would be ridiculous.

Then what is it?

It is the candid confession of what the Bible calls, the 'natural man'; who, by nature, is vitally, essentially, consistently interested in himself and his concerns; who is, in the plainest sense, self-interested. All else follows from this basic fact.

The dominant thought in the paragraph quoted, is that of self-interest, self-aggrandisement. Nothing else figures. No-one else figures. The main idea is to get to the top of the tree. There's no thought of bending those blazing energies to help somebody else up at the same time, unless as an incidental side effect of the main exercise—to get Sir Gerald to the top, and to stay there.

Does this sound a harsh, censorious judgement? I don't intend it as such. This is simply a statement of fact.

Sir Gerald, with characteristic honesty, is pointing us not only to himself but ourselves. This is the way most men are. Extroverts or introverts, public figures or private citizens, bold or retiring, we are all of us by nature disposed to allow self-interest to push and prod us into action,

[1] Ron Goldman (ed.), *Breakthrough*, p. 159.

to take what we can, make what we can, whenever we can, however we can; and devil take the hindmost. Self-interest squats on the throne and dictates our pattern of life, to an enormous degree.

For the majority of men, self-interest means whatever ministers to our ease and comfort: bodily, social, even spiritual. For others self-satisfaction will only be gained by the achievement of popularity, adulation, power: and this passionate drive will oust the more sluggish urges of self. But self will be still in command, still providing the main, habitual dynamic, all the same.

> *Fame is the spur that the clear spirit doth raise*
> (*That last infirmity of noble minds*)
> *To scorn delights, and live laborious days.*[1]

The *clear spirit*, mark you; the singleminded spirit. Milton knew his human nature. A rather different writer—a talented novelist of our day, Howard Spring—shrewdly chose that evocative phrase, *Fame is the Spur*, as the symbolic title of a magnificent story. It concerned the rise of a richly gifted youth, Hamer Shawcross, from humblest beginnings in working class Ancoats, to the splendour of a national reputation, crowned with a viscountcy and a seat in the Lords, via the Commons and the Cabinet. In his, oh so typical inner life, the mixed motives of self-service and service to the common weal—to right wrong, to fight for justice and dignity for the worker—jostled each other side by side. The real tragedy is played out as the subtle temptation to lose his passionate idealism, and to settle for fame and status, slowly gains the upper hand. The outward man is a brilliant success. The inner man is an inglorious failure. It is a powerful, sympathetic novel; and a penetrating one. It is a story about human nature. It divides the joint and marrow of what goes on in a man's inmost being.

---

[1] Milton, *Lycidas.*

How can we stop it happening? How can we reverse the process? We read such stories, we look at life around us, and, as we gaze deeply, we are sometimes wryly amused, but far more often horrified and appalled, to discover what a dissembler man is; how ingeniously he cloaks his real character under such splendid camouflage; doing such excellent things, all too often, for such tawdry reasons.

We smile indulgently at the small child who becomes astonishingly biddable a few days before Christmas or his birthday . . . yet he is in fact very akin to his elders but not betters; to the waiter whose obsequious politeness may well spring from his hope of a generous tip and not at all, in truth, from the grace of God which Hilaire Belloc said often lay in courtesy. And what of the man who remains honest because, by nature unscrupulous, he knows that a bad reputation will ruin his chances of profit? Is he a rare creature or is his name legion? And how many of us are misers who would be in anguish to lose the social esteem of our peers, and so with secret regret, have to pay our modest way? How many of us have offered time and talent to help others not so much out of compassion but, because within the circle of our benevolence, we find chance to let out the secret exhibitionist within, on a highly respectable and very long leash. We can strut and preen ourselves with discretion, at the same time exercising our itch for power and/or admiration.

In all such cases, self is as firmly established as the mainspring motive as in the case of the rascal-judge in Jesus' parable, who frankly admitted he cared nothing for God or justice, and was only moved to settle a case because the determined lady plaintiff was wrecking his siestas.

So . . . who then *can* be saved? as the disciples once despairingly asked their Lord. It was a not altogether unrelated occasion.

A would-be disciple, wealthy, well-bred, eager, apparently urged on by a passion for life of the highest quality—pure in heart, we might say—had turned away nerveless from the prospect of taking to the roads, penniless, with this strangely fascinating but impecunious vagrant preacher, having suddenly, humiliatingly discovered that his quest wasn't as pure and whole-hearted as he had imagined it was.

Who then can be saved? Who can become truly, characteristically, habitually pure in heart? Who can disinherit self and pride, and live for God alone?

I always imagine Jesus nodding his entire agreement with their bewilderment at this point. He is with them all the way.

With men, he says, this is impossible. But with God, all things are possible.

> *The most impossible of all,*
>   *Is, that I e'er from sin should cease;*
> *Yet shall it be, I know it shall:*
>   *Jesus, look to Thy faithfulness!*
> *If nothing is too hard for Thee,*
> *All things are possible to me.*

> *All things are possible to God,*
>   *To Christ, the power of God in man,*
> *To me, when I am all renewed,*
>   *When I in Christ am formed again,*
> *And witness, from all sin set free,*
> *All things are possible to me.*[1]

Yes, but there's another question, hard on the heels of the first, demanding to be answered.

Why on earth should anyone start to try for this dizzy height? If purity of heart is so Himalayan an achievement, why concern yourself with it? Why attempt the virtually impossible, at all?

[1] Charles Wesley.

This is the point at which argument is abortive, if not silly. Experience must take over. The answer is there, waiting to be found. But you must widen your horizons, if you wish to find it.

The answer confirmed itself again, gloriously, in my mind, only the other day, in reading a newspaper feature; penned by a journalist who had been moved more deeply than he cared almost to admit; describing tersely what he had seen in Calcutta, observing at first hand the work of an extraordinary band of Christian women led by a little Albanian in her sixties—Mother Theresa. You will have heard of her, no doubt. She first went out to India, an eighteen year old postulant to the Irish Loreto sisterhood. She found that prayer and meditation were simply insufficient in the face of the appalling suffering all around her, and was moved to a new adventure of grace and sacrifice which continues to this day. It has proved her life work, and it is now well known—and rightly so. You may perhaps remember her some time ago, on television, in a vivid programme lighting up the enterprise for which she has been responsible, in twenty-four branch houses of her Missionary sisterhood now spread across India.

This is what the newsman said. When you have heard it you will understand why I venture to quote so fully.

He begins by reporting that somebody had crudely daubed the wall of the convent run by Mother Theresa, with the hammer, sickle and star of the communist party now governing the city and West Bengal. Then he goes on:

If any Communist can offer as much disinterested care as the sisters then he can have my vote at any election he asks for it. For three days the sisters let me watch them at work and it is a heart-breaking, stomach-turning and awesome experience.

Watch them in the orphanage just up the road, handling new-born babies shaped and sized like wizened rats, and you see sheer gentleness in action. See them coping with the queues at the dispensary, where a German doctor-sister is inoculating, plastering and drugging for hours on end, dripping with sweat, and you know inexhaustible patience. Then go to the leper colony, a whole shanty-town of it, beyond the stinking Entally slaughterhouse, and observe calm in the face of horror.

But to discover the heart of their vocation you have to go down to Kalighat, where the goddess is propitiated each day by the slaughter of animals at a block in an open courtyard. Alongside it is the stone shed of Nirman Hirday. The sisters bring the unwanted dying off the streets to this place so that they will know that somebody cares about their last few hours or days. To anybody who does not care it must seem a useless exercise. but in Calcutta it is terribly important. Old men with skin more fragile than tissue paper stretched over their chicken bones lie here mute and inert with glazed eyes, while a nun changes the dressings on rancid sores. Old women dribble and squitter incontinently from their stretcher beds all over the floor, and a sister rustles up with a smile (a smile!) to mop up the mess. You go to Nirman Hirday in a temperature of 104 degrees F. with 90 per cent humidity, expecting a smell compounded of rotting flesh and disinfectant. In fact, the place is immaculate and you cannot catch any odour at all . . . There is just Mother Theresa and her sisters working a miracle of love. . .[1]

And your reaction to that . . . ?

One, no doubt, is to take, as it were, the shoes from off your feet; for the place you are standing on, in mind and imagination, is holy ground.

And why?

Because you feel, deeply, without hesitation, and by divine instinct, that this is the state of mind and the style of life, to which you and every man were once called;

[1] Geoffrey Moorhouse,'Faith, Hope and Leprosy', in The *Guardian*, April, 1969.

to which you are still called; which involves that complete forgetfulness of self leading, for love's sake, straight to the sacrifice of all things in your needy neighbour's interest. You sense a compulsive attraction towards this sort of Christlike magnificence, so divested of selfish ease and the overtones of pride; so truly, fully, gloriously loving; so fully human, so divine.

I, if I be lifted up, said Jesus, will draw all men unto me. I believe he was speaking of what you now feel, listening to this testimony of his power and spirit at work in the world today.

Where else, but in continued exuberant devotion to Christ, have these Missionaries of Charity, as they are so unerringly called, discovered the mainspring of their purity of heart, and the fullness of joy they undoubtedly know, and which was reflected in the unforgettable features of Mother Theresa?

And to whom else save Christ, do they in turn point you and me, bidding us believe that what is possible for two hundred ordinary women in India, is, by the same token, gloriously possible for all the human race who will?

Our Lord did not say: 'How happy are the pure in heart, for they shall see God, and what a pity it is that in this lost and sinful world, nobody can ever manage to do so.'

If that had been the sum and substance of his teaching, it is safe to say that the world would have ignored Jesus from the beginning. There have always been more than enough maddeningly elusive wills-o-the-wisp taunting the longing hearts of men. But in the light of Nirman Hirday, and what Mother Theresa and her band of ordinary women made extraordinary by the grace of our Lord Jesus Christ are doing there, who dare shrug his shoulders and dismiss the Gospel promise as shadow without substance? Who, recalling other great ones, the names of others like her, from Francis to Schweitzer, from Ida Scudder to Martin Luther King, of whom the world was not worthy, who in their life, and death, testified to the power of grace to purify the miserably stained heart of man—who, I repeat, in the light of their testimony dare deny the reality of the Gospel power to purify the heart, redeem the life, and show forth man truly come of age, truly God-like? Especially, when, remembering these citizens of the New Age, we feel again the ache of longing, the irresistible sense that this, too, is what we were born for: to lose the stain of self and put on the beauty of Christ within.

Hear again—and disbelieve at your peril and to your sorrow, a sorrow like that of the Rich Young Ruler's—the Gospel proclamation: that God was in Christ, reconciling us egotists to himself, by the simple process of giving us a new, a perfect heart, a heart from self set free, at the cost of yielding our wills to his: adventuring upon a commitment, real, unfeigned, a commitment to Christ, as Way, Truth, Life; commitment which means stepping out as if all he claimed for himself was true, thereafter to discover that it is!

This is what our fathers meant by 'saving faith' in Jesus Christ—faith that his life, his death (the death of the pure in heart, who for the joy that was set before him endured the cross, despising the shame) and resurrection, gives access to the ever-present work of the Holy Spirit within, scouring, enlightening, enlivening, empowering us, ever more truly, ever more securely; making clean our hearts within us, as we seek ever more fully, more glorious-ly, to see Christ in our neighbour, and love him to the end . . . even though the world derides and mocks; even if we, too, are finally driven to that place where, *in extremis*, we must likewise cry 'Father, forgive them . . .!' knowing that we may also cry in time or eternity 'It is accomplished!' as we yield up our spirits to him; and know the pure unutterable joy of gazing at the King in all his beauty, the fairest of ten thousand, and the altogether lovely.

> *Father of Jesus! love's reward,*
> *What rapture will it be*
> *Prostrate before Thy throne to lie,*
> *And gaze, and gaze on Thee.*

But with an infinitely more wonderful rapture than ever men gaze, lost in wonder, love and praise, before a masterpiece of eye or ear. This is what we were born for. This is the chief end of man: to glorify God in the loveliness of a life and character renewed by Christ; to know the joy unspeakable and full of glory which alone is tasted by the pure in heart; so to enter into that communion of mind and spirit with God from whom it came, and to whom it returns—which the saints have called the beatific vision; to glorify God—and enjoy him forever.

5)   Now by Chance ...

Now by chance . . . said the Master. The phrase reminded me abruptly of my friend Bill; and of the visit I paid him a while back.

When last I had seen him, he was his usual self—a physically rugged, extremely kind hearted man, a staunch ally (he and I had worked together on enterprises for youth many times—he was the sort you could utterly rely on); a firstrate husband and father of a splendid growing family.

But not now.

When I saw him now, he had been in bed for the best part of two months; since, in fact, as part of his service to the community, he had taken a party of young people abroad on holiday.

By chance he had met the son of the owner of the château in the grounds of which they were camping.

By chance, this son was a keen amateur pilot with his own 'plane.

He asked my friend Bill if he'd like a joyride, to view the estate from the air and spot exactly where the camp was located. The flight was enjoyable. But when the 'plane came in, an obstruction on the airfield loomed up. The young pilot couldn't avoid it. The 'plane overturned.

By chance, the pilot escaped unhurt. Bill didn't. By chance, his spinal cord was all but shattered. And when I visited my friend Bill, he was propped in a reclining position in the hospital bed, a tube in his throat, ready for connection to the machine by his side from which, night after night, the oxygen he needed to stay alive, was steadily pumped while he slept. By day, he could just manage to sustain his own respiration.

He could see me. He could hear me. He could whisper to me. But that was all he could do. That was all, humanly speaking, he would ever be able—will ever be able—to do.

For an hour we spoke together: family news; church news; and other talk—richer talk—which only two would-be disciples of Jesus can share—the sort of mingling of minds which perhaps Charles Wesley was speaking of when he taught the early Methodists to sing

Didst Thou not make us one,
That we might one remain,
Together travel on,
And bear each other's pain . . .

Then, you may remember, the verse goes on

Till all Thy utmost goodness prove,
And rise renewed in perfect love?

Aye, there's the rub.

I suppose we might well have cursed whatever gods there be, my friend Bill and I, at this monstrous chance which had ruthlessly cut short, with exquisite cruelty, his life of splendid service. But, thank God, we had been delivered from that sort of dead-end foolery. As it was, we talked with cheerfulness. But after I had left him, I wept to think of him lying there, helpless, a broken hulk of a man, and of the grim prospect ahead. It was only natural. If the Master could and did weep at the death of a beloved friend, my own tears were not out of place at the thought of the living death to which he, who was my friend, had been condemned . . . by chance.

And I began to think through this whole matter once more, of the existence of chance, in God's world; chance, which could permit devilry of this sort.

Long suffering Gideon, enduring with his people

70

calamities like ruin, starvation, terror and despair, long centuries before Jesus, put the matter in a nutshell when he asked his angelic visitor, 'Pray, sir, if the Lord is with us, why then has all this befallen us?'[1]

It's a daunting question to which everyman must try at least to give his own honest answer, sooner or later, as he travels the flinty road of faith.

Let me share mine, in the shape of three simple affirmations about chance.

The first sounds like plain stupid defiance of the sort of sombre facts of life represented by my friend Bill. I can't do better than borrow the phrase used (quite kindly) by my dear mother, about a certain lady who wanted a gentleman friend and seemed quite unable to acquire one. 'Chance is a fine thing!' she said.

It is indeed. Chance *is* a fine thing.

Why should we say that? How on earth *can* we, in the face of Bill?

The answer is convincing, if you will be patient enough to think it through; beginning with the effort to imagine our world as it might be if chance were excluded altogether. If, for instance, it was utterly certain that always and everywhere, the bad little boys would get the kicks, and the good little boys the ha'pence. That virtue would always be rewarded, and vice would always earn its retribution. And that nothing ever happened by chance everything being inflexibly geared and predestined.

I say—'Imagine such a world'—but in fact it's next door to impossible to imagine it at all. If, however, our minds can be stretched at least some way in this unthinkable direction, the fact begins to emerge, plain and sharply etched, that human beings wouldn't *be* human beings, as we know ourselves now. If fortune invariably swiftly smiled on the righteous, and agony and distress assailed the badly behaved at similar speed, then, unless you were a masochist

[1] Judges 6:13. RSV.

71

or badly balanced in other ways you would toe the line . . . for fear. You would also feel yourself imprisoned in a particularly abhorrent strait jacket, the worse for being invisible. You would cringe before the unseen whip of Big Brother, about to whistle across your shoulders at any moment. Life would be insupportable.

Indeed, life wouldn't *be* life; life, that is, as we know it. It would be the kingdom of dementia, inhabited by un-recognizable skulking creatures anxious at all costs to avoid suffering and in consequence unable to grow up to any sort of mature manhood. Indeed, manhood would be out of the question. Unless virtue is its *own* reward, our world's a howling wilderness. This takes some assimilation, but it's strictly true.

You may well think it a sensible thing, faced with an intractable child, to punish him (but with love in your heart, not petulant anger) for bad behaviour, in order to drive home the vital truth that this world is not the sort of place where anything goes; and, if he thinks it is, he is in for sore trouble later on. But you are well aware, when you administer the smack, or deprive him of his favourite pleasure for a season, that the whole operation is a purely temporary measure, designed simply to urge him on his way to respond freely to the impulse you hope and believe he feels, however erratically, to behave himself, and make a healthy, free response to the challenge life holds out, to do what's right, and reject what's wrong.

For he is living in a world in which freedom—i.e., chance in action—is utterly basic to a true understanding of who we are, what we are; basic to our capacity not only for growth, but for enjoyment, happiness, fulfilment.

Let's hold on for a moment or two longer, to our picture of people growing up.

My wife and I have two sons. Basically, there were two ways in which we could have sought to rear them. We could have tried to protect them—fully and completely. Or we could have exposed them, aptly, sensibly and naturally to hazards of a thousand kinds which, of course, is what we did.

We might have tried to protect them, thoroughly, from the fell clutch of circumstance and the bludgeonings of chance. Virtually unthinkable though it finally is, let's try to pursue this harebrained line of thought as far as we can and consider how it might have worked out.

We would certainly never have allowed them as toddlers to climb, or to play with toys, or come anywhere near fires or switches and suchlike; for obvious reasons. The safest environment would undoubtedly have been an empty, cosily padded room; fitted with an air-purifier.

They would certainly not have been allowed to go out of the house unless under strictest supervision; and, then, certainly not on to a road where traffic flowed. No car— or bus-rides—for them . . . consider the hazards! No games with other children . . . think of the risks involved! Schooling would have had to be carried out at home— for everyone knows that the chance of infection, sickness, disease in any average school is real and sometimes formidable. They would never have been allowed to . . .

But let's cut it short. The point is made. Telescope the argument. The plain conclusion is that to seek to outwit the basic human situation in which chance is the main planking, is to destroy the growth of personal freedom, which makes humans *human*. It is to close the door to true personal growth and development. A child brought up in such a completely monstrous atmosphere would probably piteously rebel, then finally degenerate into a tragically stunted, crazed and sub-human creature, dwarfed in mind and spirit, unspeakably frustrated. He would not, could not, experience normal health and happiness. He would end by going mad—quietly, or savagely. Have you ever seen the unhappy, bitter or insufferable product of a home where there has been *too much* care and protection?

Putting the matter positively, the fact is that to expose a child to the normal chances and changes of this mortal life, is the necessary prelude to any sort of maturity. Common sense of course dictates that in infancy and small childhood, especially protective care is vital; but only and strictly as a passing phase. To expose a child to situations without number, day after day, in which he may get hurt— badly hurt—is the completely necessary condition whereby you give him, at the same time, *the chance to be himself*— to grow, to achieve, to become a person in his own right: to taste the exhilarating joys and infinite fulfilment we know life was designed to afford; and *must* afford, unless we are to twist and batter it wretchedly out of shape.

Chance, I repeat, is a fine thing. This is why. What is more (if you are convinced by this kind of argument) this is also why it's meaningless—though oh, how very, very understandable—to cry out in bitter resentment, when accidents happen, when the worst befalls: 'Why should this sort of thing be allowed to happen?' If this is a world in which freedom is basic to human experience—the sort of world in which only on the basis of personal freedom, the unfettered swing and interaction of events, we have the chance to grow up, to become human beings, to discover untold delight and enchantment—then it's also the sort of world in which, if we're honest, we simply *have* to learn (however fearsomely hard it may be at times) to take the rough with the smooth; to take our chance, with all that that may involve alike of unspeakable sadness or heavenly joy.

You could, presumably, have a world—and, if you believe in God, presumably the choice confronted even him, in his creative majesty—where nothing would be permitted to introduce the cutting edge of sorrow; a world where you were effectively prevented from exposure to the risk of both success and failure; tragedy and triumph; heaven or hell; delight or disaster. But if you were a human being, you would find such a world a nightmare place to live: far, far more so than you find this present one.

The more one thinks about it, the clearer it becomes that if chance wasn't an ever-present reality, the ground bass, to the infinitely varied and varying symphony of life, then there wouldn't be any music at all—joyous, inspiring or sombre. As it is, remember, in all fairness to the Creator that, for the most part, the ten million million chances to which we are all subject every day for good or ill, *work out well;* or at least, bring no intolerable calamity in their train.

Chance, then, is the ocean upon which the frail vessel of our lives journeys; a heaving ocean, subject to hurricanes and cross currents now and then; but, for the most part, an ocean permitting vast numbers of folk the possibility of a satisfying voyage.

Which brings me immediately to the second of my reminders. Chance is a fine thing, we said, but it is not the *only* thing.

By which we mean . . . ?

Well, to follow the same figure, if chance is the ocean upon which we embarked, each vessel afloat is equipped— at the start, at least—with a rudder. We are not condemned to drift, hapless and helpless, unless we want it that way.

> *To every man there openeth*
> *A way, and ways, and a way . . .*

Exactly. And every man 'decideth the way his soul shall go'.

How?

By the exercise, for good or ill, of that divinely inbuilt endowment—his will.

Will is the factor which can take and use the chances

and changes of this mortal life one way or another. Life is saying—'Take your chance! Make the best of your chances!' By which it means—assert yourself! Master your circumstances! Work to a pattern! Life is what you make it—not blind chance!

But, of course, as one swiftly goes on to realize, what matters supremely—and what I want to emphasize—is that in the fulfilment of plan and pattern it is the quality of the will—the *moral* quality, the inner fibre of a person—that matters. What the man is like—what sort of man he is—proud, vain, contemptuous, arrogant, indifferent, unfriendly, or compassionate, humble, gentle, patient, courageous. What description he answers to is going to make all the difference, in the short as well as the long run, to what he makes of his chances; how he deals with the openings life offers him; and—most important, from the point of view of Bill and all those in his gallant company—what he makes of life when, through mischance, all seems lost.

(That very word 'mischance' incidentally might give us food for thought. It's interesting that when we want to emphasize the sombre side of chance, we must devise a special word to do it—a word clearly implying that the ordinary working of chance is intended to be, is assumed to be, benevolent or at least neutral, not malevolent.)

Now by chance . . . a certain priest came down that way. So did the Levite. Both were estimable characters, who undoubtedly were in the habit of paying twenty shillings in the pound, not breaking their word, and doing what duty clearly demanded. But at root, they were self-willed: in this instance, clearly illustrated in the way in which, by sensible deduction, we may easily imagine them obeying the prime law of self-preservation and scuttling for safety. Chance offered them a splendid opening. Neither took it. But, equally by chance, a Samaritan came where the man lay beaten and broken. He got off his beast, and succoured the victim. Into the world of blind chance, goodwill—mark the word! — began to operate as a saving, redemptive, purposeful, potent factor. It always does. It is God's way with the raw material of chance; goodwill always operates on the loom of life to produce the warp and weft of a splendid pattern, meaningful, satisfying, a thing of beauty which is a joy to God and man.

It's over half a century now since two little pitiful waifs, a small boy and his equally diminutive sister from the slums of Naples, were selling their matches on a busy square; and, by chance, accosted a young Methodist minister. Energized by that same Holy Spirit of whom the Master by implication spoke, in his unforgettable story of the Samaritan, the minister stopped to enquire further. Their mother was ill; they were homeless.

What followed was indeed the same parable of the Samaritan, re-enacted in a southern Italian setting. The mother was sought and found. The little ones were taken, with her glad consent, to the shelter of the minister's modest home. His wife was—to say the least—startled; but like ladies of the manse in ten thousand places, responded with that graceful versatility for which ten thousand ministers have daily cause to thank God.

And that was the start of the Casa Materna story;[1] a rich, virtually incredible romance of faith and compassion. From those virtually accidental beginnings, there has sprung one of the most astonishing enterprises in modern Christendom; a Protestant Home for 180 homeless children. 'Casa Materna' means 'The House with the Mother's Heart'. Today, alongside the Home itself, is a splendid school affording day education for another 200 children. It is literally hemmed in on three sides (the fourth is the sea) by Roman Catholic schools and institu-

[1] Cyril J. Davey, *The Santi Story*, Epworth, 1966.

tions. Tolerance, understanding, gratitude and admiration have been won at home and abroad for Casa Materna over the decades, by a prodigiously faithful dedication of life, endowment and all else, of the gifted Santi family. It would be hard to parallel this romance of Christian compassion and heroism, harder to exceed it, anywhere in the western world. Thousands of erstwhile hopeless youngsters, in the fell clutch of circumstance, rescued and afforded life and growth and joy . . . by chance? Yes, but only at the start. Chance was taken by a will and heart fired and powered by the Spirit of the living Christ—and every day for over half a century mischances of life have been turned to glorious account in the economy of the Kingdom.

What we have just cited is a parable, a symbol, a setting forth of the way in which God intends every man to co-partner him in his as yet unfinished creation.

This is a world in which God intends his sons to exercise his own divine gift, freely bestowed, to shape and fashion the raw material of chance and circumstance, after his own pattern of love, beauty, harmony, truth, and joy; in which the full glory of life, indeed, is only realized as men grapple with life as it is, inspired by his Holy Spirit to an inflexible resolution to offset, in themselves, as in the world around them, the disorder, ugliness and tragedy which is the occasional, sometimes appallingly stiff price we pay for the privilege of living in a basically free world; enabled to make or mar our destiny, and our Father's purpose.

A world, what is more, in which no man need walk blindly, without assurance or example, inspiration and challenge; but, on the contrary, may find all four in the life and work, the death and rising again, of Jesus, man of Nazareth, whom men grew to recognize as strong Son of God.

By chance, he was born into a lowly home. By chance,

78

an outcast. By chance reared not at the centre of things, but in a backwoods setting of doubtful reputation; by chance (if strong tradition is to be trusted) the elder son upon whom responsibility for a widowed mother and growing brothers soon fell.

By chance a man who (when the hidden years were over, and he had received his divine summons to show himself the Man above all men, the Man for others) called men to him who proved finally neither staunch nor over-percipient; who forsook him and fled at his hour of need. By chance, a man born into an age and a society in which the Establishment was securely held by minds encrusted over with rigid traditions and inflexible loveless prejudice. By chance, a man therefore whose Good News of the timeless truth of the Father (the law of perfect love demanding to be recognized by all and ignored by none, a way to be joyously ventured upon, if the world was ever to become the Father's glory and not man's shame) was bound to be scorned and derided, rejected and destroyed for ever.

But it did not happen that way. For the divine power surged through this man, The will of the Father was his meat and drink. He said so. Men saw it was so. And at length, not by chance at all, but because he understood with unflawed divine clarity, the redemptive strategy of the Father, he deliberately laid down his life as the Good Shepherd of the sheep; finally to take it again, because it simply was not possible that death should hold him in its grip; knowing as by immense Godly insight he did that out of the revolting agony of his death, as a seed in the ground dies and fructifies, so this unspeakable tragedy might be turned to the world's good account.

So it was. Finally, in the death and resurrection of Jesus, Christians too may claim their own final insight into this matter of chance and mischance.

This is the third and last thing I wish to say. Chance is a

fine thing; but it is not the only thing. Will can direct and master chance over and again. But if the very worst (by human reckoning) happens—even the most devilish mischance *is not the final thing*.

It is a splendid thing, no doubt about it, to be of such stern stuff as to say with Henley:

> *Out of the night that covers me,*
> *Black as the pit from pole to pole,*
> *I thank whatever gods may be*
> *For my unconquerable soul.*

> *In the fell clutch of circumstance*
> *I have not winced nor cried aloud.*
> *Under the bludgeonings of chance*
> *My head is bloody, but unbowed.*

But ah! what if the fell clutch of circumstance, the bludgeonings of chance, are leaving bloody not your head, but that of another, dear to you as life itself, and over whom you agonize. What if it should be your friend? Your wife, your husband, your child? What then?

Why, mere stern stoicism, personal defiance however splendid, will not do. It serves its turn. It is magnificent. I will not scoff at it, as some Christians ineptly do. It is a pointer to the human spirit at its most dauntless. It has a Godliness all its own.

But you need something more, when the heart is breaking, at the sight of someone you care for shattered, as the wheel of life seems remorselessly, mindlessly to grind on its uncaring way to crush and destroy.

Then, only the vision of an empty tomb will do; and the remembrance of a voice that cries, 'Why seek ye the living among the dead!' and goes on to cry 'He is risen!' And an apostolic assurance bidding us rejoice in the knowledge that if we too or our loved ones suffer and die with him, we shall likewise share his resurrection power and glory.

Was it chance alone, I wonder, that caused a brave friend of mine, herself at that moment caught up in dire distress, to write me a letter and enclose this splendid poem by Constance Holm? It arrived on my desk on the very morning on which I was trying to wrestle with this theme; and says finely what only a poet—and a Christian—can say.

> The tree that fell last year knows now just why it fell
> Why came the hell
> Of axe and saw, and leaping, clear blue flame.
> To the world's uses it was set in pit, or ship
> Or polished cabinet,
> Or other needs of man.
> The spirit of the tree knows now the plan
> Of that, its agony
>
> So we, fall'n in the mire shall some day surely know
> Why life held blow on blow,
> And sacrificial fire, and knife;
> Seeing one stand the firmer for our rout,
> Or some brave, laughing ship of youth sail out
> The braver for our pain.
> So—knowing, seeing—we shall smile again
> At this our Calvary.

Only the Christian knows how to smile, at Calvary, with an echo of the mirth of the angels, which gaze on the face of the crucified and risen Lord, and adore the mystery of love which has endured the worst of life's tempests, and remained unshaken.

We once had the immense privilege of sharing our home for some months with a young couple whose golden-haired little girl of three was steadily dying, by chance, of leukaemia. My wife and I have remained the braver

81

for their pain ever since—and shall always. The agony of many weeks of hopes steadily dashed, of prayers apparently both faith-filled and unheard, at last ended; and her dainty spirit was released to that glorious unseen world, from the enheartening and intelligent contemplation of which modern man so often turns sadly and foolishly away; that world unspeakable and full of glory where the guardian angels of children do always behold the face of the Father.

There was something of the face of God in the drawn features of Daphne, the mother, as she spoke finally for her husband as well as herself, through her tears. She smiled—yes smiled!—as she said 'Well, there's one thing about it—we shall know how to comfort others who go through this experience'. And she meant it. She knew with a certainty only Christians possess, that death was the beginning, not the end of the drama of life, for her lovely little one.

She also knew the timeless truth which millions of ordinary people have found dawning, marvellously undiminished, in the darkest hour of the soul; the truth that when the music of life changes to a meaningless discordant roar, when its beauty turns to ashes, when all that's sweet turns unspeakably sour, even then, the unseen companionship of the glorified Christ holds: there is light ahead, piercing the gloom, the light of eternity.

> Leave God to order all thy ways,
>   And hope in Him whate'er betide;
> Thou'lt find Him in the evil days
>   Thy all-sufficient strength and guide:
> Who trusts in God's unchanging love
> Builds on the rock that nought can move.

And this, like Daphne and her husband, my friend Bill has discovered to be true . . . that nothing of pain and anguish, nothing in death or life, in the world as it is or

82

the world as it shall be, in the forces of the universe, in heights of horror or depths of despair, nothing in all creation can separate us from the love of God in Christ Jesus our Lord.

6) The Fiercest Test of Christian Living

THE fiercest test of Christian living . . . well, you say, there's precious little doubt about what that can be. Here comes another sermon on how to cope with life when the storm roars, the earth shakes, and your world drops to bits around you; the moment of sorrow, calamity; the moment of truth. That's the moment at which surely a man's faith is tested above all, to breaking point?

Dear me, no. I'm not thinking about such high drama at all—quite the reverse, in fact. This is a very homely, bread-and-butter-theme: which happens also to involve on occasion matters of life and death.

In precise fact, I'm thinking at the moment about a monthly series of profiles of well-known personalities I used to write years ago in our youth magazine. The necessary interviews brought me in touch with some of the most fascinating people I've ever met. I enjoyed it immensely—for the most part. Sometimes, however, very sad things were said.

I remember two outstanding people of the theatre telling me of the way in which they had been badly put off the Christian Church. At the time, as young people, both were closely associated with it. Both were at that time of life when a strong nudge in one direction or the other is enough to exercise an enormous influence which can last a lifetime.

One, a son of the manse, told me of his experience in

bed ill on one unhappy occasion, visited by an austere puritanical uncle who seized the opportunity presented by the captive nephew to read him a stern lecture on his future: how he ought to pull himself together, dedicate himself to Christ and follow in father's footsteps.

The effect was disastrous. It aroused such lively resentment in the mind of the gifted young teenager that then and there, he confessed, his growing interest in the Church was smothered under the weight of the clumsy hectoring.

Exactly the same experience was suffered by the other person, an actress of great distinction, under different circumstances. Again as a gifted teenager, with a sparkling exuberant personality, involved in amateur dramatics in her local Methodist church, she was curtly taken to task by an older woman in the church, who told the girl that the kind of make-up she wore was not at all becoming, especially for someone associated with the Church. It wasn't what one had a right to expect of a member of a church youth organisation, etc. . . .

And, the same thing happened. The girl reacted violently. She flared up. She walked out—and was lost to the Christian Church, for good. What great influence she might have had, in other, happier circumstances!

Both of which simple, significant incidents, commonplace in the extreme, point straight to my theme.

'I tell you this:' said the Master, 'there is not a thoughtless word that comes from men's lips but they will have to account for it on the day of judgement. For out of your own mouth you will be acquitted; out of your own mouth you will be condemned.'[1]

'The words that a man utters', he had just told them, 'come from the overflowing of the heart. A good man produces good from the store of good within himself; and an evil man from evil within produces evil.'[2]

[1] Matt. 12:36–37.   [2] Matt. 12:34–35.

It is the words that a man utters—especially the off-guard, casual words—that remorselessly expose his real self—good, evil, or an incongruous, often unlovely mixture of the two.

This is the fiercest test to which your Christianity is exposed and it relentlessly highlights the sham and the shoddy. It is the test to which you unthinkingly commit yourself almost every time you open your mouth. The way you handle the divine gift of speech, will declare more swiftly, accurately, devastatingly than anything else, the state of your inmost soul; healthy, or sick, good, or evil.

So . . . it won't be at all a pointless or trivial exercise, to stay for a while with this awesome thought—and let it lead us to the rediscovery of truth and wisdom in this matter; and certainly—oh, so certainly—to penitence.

How should we speak, so as to pass this most gruelling test of Christian integrity?

In two ways, at least, it seems to me; perfectly obvious—but so well worth remembering.

First, we should speak, God helping us, with reverence.

This attitude kindles afresh, and quickly, the more I think of it, the sheer wonder—nay, marvel—of human speech.

Consider what is happening, at this and every moment of our speaking together. Thought processes, in the shape I suppose of innumerable brain impulses flashing at incredible speed from brain to lungs, larynx, lips, tongue and teeth, are there being transmitted into sound waves; sound waves produced in a constantly fast-changing stream by air delicately drawn in and forced out from my body, shaped and fashioned into labials, sibilants, and the rest, and strung together in an invisible fleeting airborne cavalcade. Ceaselessly, as long as I continue speaking, that cavalcade fans out steadily into every corner of the building; so flexible, so penetrating as to be able to channel itself into every small crevice and corner; even into that tiny orifice at your temple, in orderly fashion, yet with astounding speed, with no bottleneck trouble. Not only that—the various soundwaves, arriving in strict sequence, together hold meaning for you. What you hear is not gibberish. It is coherent. You may disagree with it—you may consider it absurd. But it holds meaning for you. In a flash, the thought that I am first entertaining, then expressing in speech, is marvellously transferred and given hospitality—for the moment at least!—in your own brain cells. We share the adventure of thought, together. We pool our ideas. I seek to share with you attitudes, convictions, impressions, which, as a Christian preacher, I hope by God's grace are going to result in a larger life, added joy and freedom, for us all.

Now all this, I confess, fills me with awe and wonder, every time I stop to think about it. I marvel at the intricate brilliance, the abiding miracle, of human speech. I remember also that whatever you may fancifully or sentimentally assume about the animal creation, man alone has a gift of communication in the form of speech, which dwarfs into utter insignificance the signals exchanged by God's other creatures. Animals and birds pipe, whistle, roar, grunt, howl, bark. Man speaks. He is a universe above his nearest companions in the world of nature about him. His gift of speech is a unique, divine bestowal.

Of course, you can shrug off all this, dismiss it as sentimental meandering. Well and good—providing you find some other, better way of starting to help yourself set a watch upon your lips; and coming to appreciate, in a glib, garrulous age, what a formidable endowment you have. I recall a lambent sentence from Philip Guedella—in a book on Churchill, I think—in which he said, 'Words—their overproduction and misuse—are the stigmata of our perishing culture'. You don't forget a sentence as blistering as that! He was referring to the printed rather than the spoken word; but his stricture would have been just as true if he had been referring to the millions of words spewed out sometimes with meticulous care, but more often with frightening carelessness, over the air, from a hundred thousand radio and TV stations, day by day: and the billions upon billions of words, spoken without a second thought, by innumerable hosts of people young and old, in the course of everyday life. What a need for due care and attention!

I shall never forget my old college principal, Dr. Lansdell Wardle, expounding the attitude of extreme reverence the ancient Hebrews brought to the gift of speech, in a study of the first chapters of Genesis. They had, he said, a vivid awareness of the enormous power of speech. Words once spoken, were thought of by the Hebrews as travelling irresistibly to their destination with self-fulfilling power. How dramatically, awesomely, this idea is indeed conveyed in the first chapter of Genesis.

'And God said, "Let there be light" . . . And there *was* light.' The Word went forth with creative power to fulfil itself. To the Hebrews, said my old teacher, words were sacred. They were not to be bandied about. They were to be used always with extreme care; viewed virtually as high explosive; dangerous in the extreme when handled irreverently. An oath was irrevocable; binding. It simply *could not* be broken. A man who broke an oath, in a sense unmanned, dismembered himself. A blessing once given, could not be repeated. The word had been spoken. This is why in the familiar Old Testament story, poor old deceived Isaac could not hand out a second birthright blessing to the outraged Esau, once the sly Jacob in his disguise of skins had coaxed it out of his blind father. The words had been spoken. They could neither be recalled nor repeated. Jacob had stolen them.

All this seems remote from us, who so often sling

statements and opinions about with the least possible imagination and respect. The ancient Hebrews would have stood appalled with horror at our wantonness.

> *Four things come not back:*
> *The spoken word;*
> *The sped arrow;*
> *Time past;*
> *The neglected opportunity.*

Indeed, and indeed. The first moreover is sometimes the most important. It is a good thing, you feel, to recall the fact?

Canon Douglas Rhymes adds vivid point to all this. He tells somewhere the story of a young married girl, cashier at a restaurant in a nearby town a few miles distant from the new housing estate on which she lived. Her husband's work took him away from home for days on end. Neighbours were not slow to note, then to comment, on the fact that the girl was seen to emerge from a car, very late at night, not infrequently, when her husband was away; a car driven by a man no-one knew.

You can complete the story without effort. Careless words were whispered; then spoken. And careless talk still costs lives in peace-time as certainly as it used to do when the war-time posters were pinned up to warn us all. The girl, of course, at last got to know what was being said about her. She was a very sensitive creature. She was not only appalled. She also swiftly grew afraid to walk down the street in day-time, in anguish at the thought of what the neighbours were thinking and saying about her. She took her own life. The neighbours were shocked. But the real blow came when the truth came out. The car driver was her employer, a kindly man, who ran the girl back home on the occasions on which she had missed the last bus. There was not a blemish on the character of either of them.

Good name in man and woman, dear my lord,
Is the immediate jewel of their souls;
Who steals my purse steals trash;'tis something, nothing
'Twas mine, 'tis his, and has been slave to thousands;
But he that filches from me my good name
Robs me of that which not enriches him,
And makes me poor indeed.

The extraordinary thing about that splendid speech, as you will remember, is that Shakespeare gives it to his most loathsome villain, Iago. They are words of sage insight and lovely sensitivity; and they spring from the mouth of a ruthless, conscienceless devil in human form. Here, once again, we see the supreme art of Shakespeare—rubbing into our minds the fact that *we know already* we are playing traitor to goodness and conscience, whenever we allow ourselves to speak slanted, ill-founded, unloving words. We stand self-condemned, sinning with a high hand even as we speak. Yet we go on speaking. That is the measure of our frailty, our shame, our utter need.

I recall once hearing of an artist's impression of Hitler in the very early Munich days, before he and his demonic gang seized power. The leader was surrounded by a group of his fanatically devoted followers, hanging on every syllable, impassioned, authoritative, demanding. The picture bore a title which might almost be thought blasphemous, but which conveyed too urgent a truth to be so dismissed: 'In the beginning was the Word.'

It is, too. At the beginning of everything that is going to change human life, massively or minutely, nearer heaven, or down to hell—there is the word—meaningful, alive, going forth in power, to invade and possess, drive and initiate; whether spoken by a statesman or a Sunday School teacher, a head of state or a housewife, a field marshal or a father. In the beginning is the word. But even before the word, the thought. And shaping the thought, the spirit; the inmost, central heart and core of a man—

self-loving or compassionate; dedicated to self-gratification or to serving one's neighbour. And the words that a man utters come from the overflowing of that heart.

I tell you this . . . there is not a thoughtless word that comes from men's lips but they will have to account for it . . .

It's worth noting that those words of Jesus follow the nastiest, and also the most stupid smear, launched against him. 'It's only by the prince of the devils that this man drives the devils out', they had sneered, unthinkingly.

It wasn't just the illogical silliness that was the worst feature of the jibe. It was the naked hatred which overflowed into the words. Whether they thought Jesus was right or wrong, nothing could excuse representatives of a religion whose golden law talked about loving God with all one's heart and strength, and one's neighbour as oneself, of wilfully thumbing their noses in derision at that law, and saying, in effect, and to bring some relief to the smart of their own resentment of him, 'You devil!' Knowing, as they said it, they spoke of one whom they knew, deep down, was a man from heaven, not hell. This was to stand truth on its head; deliberately to opt for the false, instead of the true; to reveal that the one they were worshipping and serving, at the deepest depth, wasn't God at all—but their own proud ego; symbolized in their status, their reputation for zeal and fidelity to their nation's faith and tradition; the awe and esteem in which they were held by common sinful folk. Real communion, life-changing, love-begetting, between them and the Father, just didn't exist. When they prayed, they prayed within themselves, like the Pharisee in the parable, with a cheap and flyblown thankfulness that they were not as other men, but a sight better.

It all came out in their words, first. Their speech betrayed them; not as Peter's thick accent did by the fire in the Temple courtyard, after the arrest in the Garden,

91

but in the contempt, the arrogance, the wilful unloveliness of their words. They spilled out, quick, hot, evil, faithfully testifying to the devilry within.

A man who talks the way they did, has put himself out of reach of forgiveness. He has barred the door to any gracious invasion of the Spirit.

Stand back a little. Remember. Reflect. Try to recall the quality of your offguard, unguarded speech. What overall impression do you give of the real man within?

Have you a lively, Godly awareness that the Father's divine gift of speech is never to be taken in hand lightly or thoughtlessly, but reverently, discreetly, with due care and attention?

There is scarcely a better, handier thing you could do, and millions like you to improve the prospects of the Kingdom of Christ around you and within, than to develop a splendid discipline in the matter of the words you use. They come from the overflowing of your heart; especially whenever they are tinged with feeling of any sort. When you are roused, does care and discretion begin to vanish like smoke in the wind? Is reverence forgotten?

It is very likely to be, unless that reverence, springing from a lively awareness of the power of speech, is linked inseparably to an ever greater master principle.

Let Paul state it for us.

'We are no longer to be children,' he says, 'tossed by the waves and whirled about by every fresh gust of teaching, dupes of crafty rogues and their deceitful schemes. No, let us speak the truth in love; so shall we fully grow up into Christ.'[1]

So we shall.

Speak the truth in love . . . again, there's the rub; there's the fiercest test. Who emerges from it unscathed?

A letter of complaint arrived a while back from a lady

[1] Eph. 4:14–15.

living near our church. It seemed wholly justified. Some of our Sunday morning worshippers, it appeared, had acquired the habit of parking their cars, not only outside her house, but also in front of her drive-in. She herself was a car-owner, and worshipper at another church in the neighbourhood. She had been prevented from going out by these thoughtless folk.

I went round to see her; and found her, so far as one could judge, a fair-minded and tolerant person. She told me candidly and without heat, what her experience had been.

'The thing that really shook me', she said, 'was that when I went out to speak to the people responsible, they actually seemed to resent my telling them! I almost felt as though I had committed the nuisance!'

I was sad, but not surprised. I know my own marked ability to react hastily, nastily, to the suggestion that I am silly or irresponsible.

Speak the truth in love . . . well, I imagined the lady had done. But even if she had sounded annoyed (as she had every right to be) what justification for resentment could there possibly be?

What acute subtle challenges everyday life presents us with! How many slippery surfaces to put the skids suddenly under our self-control and amiability! Is there a fiercer test of ultimate Christian loving integrity, than the words that well up from the depths of our hearts—when our consciences have been pricked, our pride hurt?

This is often the moment of truth—all the more important because it is so ordinary, mundane, trivial; entirely unaccompanied by glamour, heroism, sacrifice. Just an encounter between people, slightly or deeply at variance. One is right; the other wrong. Or maybe both are right, each in a different way; contending for a viewpoint, a course of action, quite justifiable, sensible. How fearfully easily umbrage is taken, an atmosphere builds up, or the temperature cools. How natural! How sad! How faithless!

But how glorious, how infinitely joyous and rewarding when the victory *is* won, the truth *is* spoken—and heard—in love. The gospel of reconciliation then shines out in its own peculiar splendour.

Some time ago in the chair of a hard-working committee, I judged it right to criticize an action of a group of youth workers at my church. Like a good many chairmen of meetings, I did the job hamfistedly. If not a sledgehammer, at least a fourteen pounder was used to crack the nut.

The leader of the organization sat quietly throughout. Next day, after a sleepless night, as he told me, he came round to see me. I had distressed him. But he didn't let his distress fester. He came to talk the thing out. He spoke gently, carefully. He felt responsible, he told me, for the action I had criticized. He thought it had been dealt with already. He could only therefore assume that I had for some inscrutable reason, wanted to imply a basic dissatisfaction with his leadership. (Does anybody here recognize the situation? But of course! This scene has been played out a hundred times within the life of many a community.)

Ah! but this tension was resolved. My friend had grown up in Christ. He spoke the truth in love. Not a petulant word was said. Honesty, yes—plenty of it, but no acrimony. My friend had come to unburden himself—another man might have accused and upbraided. My friend came to explain and to seek an explanation, to inform. He had one altogether Christian end in view; mutual understanding and reconciliation.

At the end of our talk—during which I of course was given ample, gracious opportunity to make amends for my clumsy contribution to the committee—both of us were closer together than before. There was relief and thankfulness in both our hearts, a danger briskly avoided;

not this time to life and limb, but the risk of fracturing something more precious still—a healthy relationship.

And what, with gracious effectiveness, did my friend do? He demonstrated, as his life so often does, that in his inmost soul, there dwells the spirit of love—which holds his tongue in check, and permits him only to speak, when doubts and tensions rise, words which make peace, not strife.

Your Christian role is precisely the same.

You cannot stop the fighting in Biafra, or Vietnam, or wherever. But in your lifetime if you are similarly a man of grace, controlled by Christ, you will prevent a hundred ugly little wars from ever flaring up at all, right where you are—by exercising the ministry of reconciliation, by speaking the truth in love, Christian love, the love which Paul describes in that superb paragraph from one Corinthians thirteen, a paragraph which gets to the heart and core of personal Christianity.

'This love of which I speak is slow to lose patience—it looks for a way of being constructive . . . it does not cherish inflated ideas of its own importance. Love has good manners and does not pursue selfish advantage. It is not touchy . . . knows no end to its endurance, no end to its trust, no fading of its hope: it can outlast anything . . .'

This is the spirit which will not only choose the words which heal and do not hurt, but knows full well—and acts on the knowledge—that it is not only the 'what' but also the 'how' that matters enormously, in the matter of speaking the truth in love.

It's not what you say, it's the way that you say it! The line of an old jazz hit from many years ago, is accurate to a degree. Tone, pitch, tempo—all these make up the setting in which love speaks in hi-fi terms, authentic, undistorted: or else the exercise breaks down. Without genuine love, an apology can be turned into a renewed insult, an expression of thanks turned into a contemptuous mockery, words outwardly warming turned into a message that chills to the bone.

Desmond Morris, zoologist, makes this point neatly in his absorbing book *The Naked Ape*; banned, I gather, in some countries—and not altogether to one's surprise, since it cuts man down to size, strips him of most of his pretensions, and underlines his most intimate and sometimes hilarious relationship to the rest of the animal creation.

As an off beat but thorough Lenten exercise in proper Christian humility, I commend the book heartily. The point I wish to stress, however, is not on this main theme, but on a minor, but fascinating aspect of man-animal communication, in which the importance of what Morris calls 'Mood Talking' is discussed. He remarks on the fact that in dealing with animals, words are not even as important, but in hard fact much less important than the tone of voice used. To put the matter beyond doubt, he invites you to try cooing 'Bad dog!' at your pet, and to snarl 'Good dog!'; and see what reactions you produce. You only have to use your imagination a moment to envisage what would happen.

The words that a man utters come from the overflowing of the heart . . . indeed they do . . . not only the selection, but the sound—kind, sympathetic, enheartening; cold, aloof; or burning with anger. Whatever they are, however they are spoken—they wing their way with power; and fulfil their ministry, for good or ill.

I well remember a church member coming to speak to me in great distress. She had just witnessed an ill-tempered exchange between worshippers who had emerged only minutes before from a communion service.

'How they can say such things to each other after just coming out of church!' she cried in anguish.

Ah, but they can! And they do!

96

'The man who never says a wrong thing is a perfect character', remarked the apostle James[1] with commendable accuracy. And, really warming to a subject he obviously knew a good deal about, he went on, 'What a huge stack of timber can be set ablaze by the tiniest spark! And the tongue is in effect a fire . . . Beasts and birds of every kind . . . have been subdued by mankind; but no man can subdue the tongue. It is an intractable evil, charged with deadly venom. We use it to sing the praises of our Lord and Father, and we use it to invoke curses upon our fellow-men who are made in God's likeness . . . My brothers, this should not be . . .'[2]

Indeed it should not. But there are a thousand ways in which a man may swiftly feel, then express, a sense of annoyance, anger. You have only to invade his privacy, threaten his rights, strip him of a tiny slice of comfort, cast never so faint a doubt on his shining motives, and he is ready to square up to you, aggrieved, nine times out of ten.

But . . . the Christian is the tenth; or should be. We know it. And, again and again, we fail to fill the role. This is why this theme makes most of us squirm, starting with the preacher.

Is there any open secret to proficiency in the supreme art of speaking the truth in love; in holding one's tongue, and keeping a watch over one's lips?

If there is; if anyone knows of an easy formula for keeping the peace, and making the peace, let him speak, without delay!

I know of none.

All I know is that I seek to follow a Master who will not cease from reminding me of my desperate need in this matter, and who himself provides the example, again and again, in the Gospel story. I realize, watching his words and deeds as closely as I may, and feeling again and again

[1] James 3:2.   [2] James 3:5–10.

97

the overwhelming sense that I am eavesdropping not upon some imaginary, artfully contrived literary invention, but upon a slice of real-life experience which could not have been invented, that I am in the presence of the Master of words, as well as deeds.

Moreover, he was not by nature 'gentle Jesus, meek and mild'—in the sense of one too good to be true, and shrinking, anxious at all costs never to give offence, eager to please everybody. Rather do I find (first to my satisfaction and later, to my shame) one who was in all points tempted like as I am, yet without sin. Here was no faceless, innocuous, impassive cypher of a human being. Here was a passionate man, whose earnestness and intensity make our emotional life seem pale and shadowy by contrast: a vigorous initiator, a radical, a swift challenger, a fearless champion; who was swift to expose evil and sham, wherever he found it; indeed a man of anger, of stern words, yet with such a holy difference from my wretched tantrums! For his righteous indignation *was* righteous, through and through. Mine is so sadly, so frequently, unrighteous resentment, rooted and grounded, not in the sheer selfless love of God and goodness and the true life and liberty of one's neighbour— as his was—but generated out of a sorry, squalid love of self, a well-developed and sensitively skinned ego, a well-nourished care for my own rights, status, prestige.

So that his anger and mine, his words and mine, are for the most part worlds away from each other. His words of grace and compassion, always and everywhere, forever sought to awaken a man to his true destiny and stature, rouse him to his danger, encourage him to attempt the steep ascent of love for neighbour. His words of anger burned, but with a clean flame, with no smoky undertones of self and pride. Always they are called forth by outrage done to fellow men, and so to the Father; never to himself.

98

Equally, when he himself was the target for vengeful jeers, sneers, slanders and abuse, from the throats of hollow men whose lovelessness stood exposed in the light of his presence, he held his peace. If he challenged their words, it was not to get even with them. It was to defend and expound the truth, the whole truth, and nothing but, which he still spoke in love.

Thus Peter, in one of the shortest yet most memorable pen portraits of Jesus, could say of him:

'He committed no sin, he was convicted of no falsehood; when he was abused he did not retort with abuse, when he suffered he uttered no threats, but committed his cause to the One who judges justly . . .'[1] It is for you to follow in his steps . . .

A little later, he returns to make that last point again, in language as perfect as it is lucid.

'To sum up:'—he says—'be one in thought and feeling, all of you; be full of brotherly affection, kindly and humble-minded. Do not repay wrong with wrong, or abuse with abuse; on the contrary, retaliate with blessing . . .

'Whoever loves life and would see good days
must restrain his tongue from evil
and his lips from deceit;
must turn from wrong and do good,
seek peace and pursue it . . .'[2]

Retaliate with blessing . . . what a magnificent Christian slogan! Yet another of the imperishable phrases to come from the treasury of the New English Bible, giving us exactly the stance, the clue, the starting point we need, in our quest after holiness—true, glowing health and wholeness—of word and thought.

And *how* do we start?

Why, in exactly the same way as we start to become

[1] I Pet. 2:22–23. [2] I Pet. 3:8–11.

proficient in any other strenuous art and discipline. Namely, bit by bit, day by day. An accomplished actor does not learn his craft in six easy lessons, but by determination, dedication, deep, sustained, sacrificial. So can the Christian, in the still greater art of speaking not with simulated passion or controlled eloquence, but with the universal accent of love, overflowing, from a heart of goodness.

Forgive me quoting Peter yet again—but in the very last verse of the letter from which comes the shining truth already quoted, he puts the truth in three short words of admonition and advice. This is how the letter ends.

'Grow', he says, 'in the grace and in the knowledge of our Lord and Saviour Jesus Christ. To him be glory now and for all eternity!'

A rather more telling finish, one ventures to think, than a trite 'Yours sincerely'!

Grow in grace . . . there's the secret.

If I felt that, having been born with a quick tongue and a low boiling point, I was condemned forever to let my tongue run away with me, the ground would be cut from under my feet, as a preacher. I do not believe this to be true. On the contrary, I believe with all my heart that *everyman can learn to grow in grace*. Bit by bit, inch by laborious inch, he can learn so to unbar the door of mind and will, personality and feeling, to the gracious invasion of God in Christ, that old habits die, old tendencies wither, and even the tongue can be tamed and sweetened.

'If any man be in Christ,' cried Paul, 'he is a new creature: old things are passed away; behold, all things are become new.'[1]

And they *can* become new! New ways of thinking, of speaking, of viewing our fellows. The Christian is born again, into a new world in which he is nourished upon,

[1] 2 Cor. 5:17. A.V.

and seeks to nourish those around him upon the sort of love first seen in Christ, which so gripped Paul that he was able to describe it so faultlessly in his first Corinthian letter.

Yes, I know. You know your fatal weakness. You speak, then think; instead of the other way round. Again and again you blurt out the unloving, bruising word. Again and again, you know with hot shame you have betrayed the cause and crucified the Son of Man afresh upon a spiky little cross erected by your own incorrigibly self-willed heart.

So do I. And for my part, thinking upon this fiercest of all the daily tests of Christian living, I find myself wanting to kneel where the woman once knelt, taken in adultery; such a common, if spectacular fault. It at least has the doubtful virtue of being interesting. But what glamour rests upon my shabby words, my loveless little scraps of self-pity and complaint? None at all.

I find myself, therefore, wanting to kneel, in mind and imagination, before the Master who has faithfully promised to hold me steady and keep company with me, if I will abide his hand in mine; and hear him say, over and above my contrition, I do not condemn you; go, and sin no more. Keep your tongue from evil and your lips from speaking deceit. Depart from evil and do good, seek peace and pursue it. My strength is sufficient for you. I will put a new heart in you—my heart—a heart of goodness. Behold, I stand at the door and knock . . .

Even so, come into my heart, Lord Jesus.

Let the words of my mouth and the meditation of my heart be acceptable in thy sight, O Lord, my Strength and my Redeemer!

7) Dinner at Simon's

A Study in Sensitivity

ONE DAY a stranger strode without warning into a class-room in Johannesburg where a class of boys were taking a matriculation aptitude test. Without ceremony, he ordered two boys to cease work and leave the room.

They were not mischief makers, rebels, anti-social misfits. They were perfectly well behaved; in fact, exemplary pupils, known and liked by their form mates.

But they were Chinese.

The man was from the Department of Labour. He was there to see that at whatever cost, however tragically absurd, white supremacy was upheld.

'The tests which we have are for whites only,' he said. 'It would be unfair to test Chinese in this way, because the results would be unreliable.'[1]

The other boys in the class, it was reported, were shocked and distressed at the treatment given to their friends; treatment clearly designed to bar them from the sort of educational advancement which would keep them on a par later on with the other boys, all Europeans.

Alas, those other boys will learn by and by, not to be so tender, so sensitive to the feelings and aspirations of those they will be taught to recognize as basically inferior to the European races: that is, unless they learn the open secret of Christian sensitivity.

Just about the same time, I read of an African woman,

[1] The *Guardian*, 14 July 1970.

again in Johannesburg, who had lately lost her husband; curtly advised by the authorities to leave the city. Why? Oh, just that African widows are not allowed to stay in urban areas. The law says so. Not just the law of the land making an ass of itself; but law which, in the hands of heartless, insensitive men, can decree sickening, inhuman injustice.

'I can't understand why my client is being punished because her husband died,' wrote a lawyer to the Government official who had ordered the widow to get out of town.[1]

Somehow, I seemed to get a whiff of the same unpleasant loveless odour, reading those snippets of information, as I did the day before, reading an account of a service conducted by the Reverend Ian Paisley, in which he had interceded with the Lord on behalf of those he called with graceless insensitivity 'Roman idolators'; and others suffering from what he identified in prayer as 'the cancer of Anglicanism'. The report seemed almost to justify William Rushton's television aside about the same redoubtable character—'Mr. Paisley is indeed a God-fearing man—God's terrified of him!'

Joking apart, however, this is a theme worth studying. It sent me back straightway, to that so strange dinner party at Simon's.[2]

It was startlingly different, this dinner-party, from our discreet, decorous and extremely private parties, held (naturally) behind closed doors, and nobody turning up uninvited.

True, only the invited guests to such affairs got down (literally) to the business of eating, reclining on their elbows, eastern fashion, in the open courtyard. Passers-by, from the street beyond, could drift in and stand around, savouring the conversational fare for the mind even if

[1] The *Guardian* 16 July 1970.　　[2] Luke 7: 36–50.

they were obliged to go without the actual delicacies being served to the guests.

This, presumably, would be the order of the day when it was noised abroad that the personality of the moment, Jesus of Nazareth, was expected to dine at Simon the Pharisee's. Those who knew what was what, expected something out of the ordinary to happen. It often did, when Jesus was present.

They were not disappointed.

One way or another, the dinner could hardly be written off as a dull and stuffy affair. What with the extraordinary business of the town harlot edging her way in right at the start, fussing over the visitor's feet almost as if he was a special client of hers . . . and then promptly howling her head off, to everybody's startled embarrassment save Jesus . . . then his exchange of conversation with Simon, his Pharisee host . . . with an unforgettable story about a couple of debtors and a moneylender thrown in for good measure . . . finally the woman, astonishingly sobered up and self-controlled again, being sent away radiant and with a look of unutterable—well, *tranquillity* would be the word (if it wasn't so absurd) on her face . . . and Jesus actually telling her her sins were forgiven because she was such a good lover . . . well!

Dinner at Simon's was a date to remember.

It happened over nineteen hundred years ago. I found myself thinking about it again the other day, not only because of the incidents I mentioned a minute ago, but equally because somebody I know very well got a slight shock at Waterloo Station—and the circumstances, and the incidents, keyed in perfectly, if sadly, together.

My friend was seeing somebody off on a boat train: a distinguished Christian minister from overseas, highly cultured, charming, a man holding high office in his Church. He had been in England on a hectic round of delegation visits and meetings—so hectic, indeed, that he hadn't even managed a couple of hours leisure at the right time of day, to take the photographs of London which he had promised to take back to his wife and family.

My friend, knowing this, had volunteered (kind soul that she is) to buy him a selection of good sightseers' views of the capital. She came along the platform armed with the pictures, and started to forage for them in her handbag, only to be met with a slightly strange request.

'I wonder, Mrs. S——,' said our overseas friend, 'if I might ask you to do something rather unusual? Would you mind allowing me please to take my seat in the train? Then, would you come along and hand over the pictures you have kindly brought me, in the compartment?'

'Why—er—yes, of course, Mr. T——, if that's what you would like me to do . . .'

'I know it sounds most odd,' said Mr. T——. 'But if you don't mind, I really think I should like you to do this. You see, some fellow countrymen of mine are already seated in my compartment. I think it might help them somewhat if they had the chance of seeing you, a white woman, treating me, an African, like a human being.'

The quiet remark stuck in my friend's mind; mine, too, when she told me of it.

I began to ponder on the background out of which it sprang. I tried hard to imagine just what lay behind the request from this shrewd and gentle African Christian. The slow, steady, hurtful years of subtle second nature pressures, felt by leaders of the community, schoolboys and widows alike, designed to re-inforce a deep un-questioning awareness into the mind of non-Europeans in the Republic of South Africa, that they were not, could never be, citizens of equal rank with their white compatriots. The rules and regulations, the social shutters and 'No admittance' signs, printed or unseen, all designed quietly, relentlessly, irrevocably to shackle Africans and Asians on a lower plane of existence—a level reserved for second class citizens. Some of them, thoughtful, talented, formidably equipped in mind and understanding, would come—*have* come—to feel an almost total frustration, intolerable and at times frantic; a frustration which could be—and is—the seedbed out of which could—and do—sprout the vigorous growths of resentment, hatred, deadly resolve; to rebel, to break out, to pay back evil for evil. The rumbling volcano which is South Africa today goes back on a stubborn, unimaginative insensitivity; an inbred incapacity, one might almost say, to regard the owner of a non-white skin, as a fellow human being.

But this insensitivity was and is of course coupled with a most delicate (indeed a hyper-) sensitivity, in the opposite, self-regarding direction. An extreme sensitivity, it is rooted in the dread of the possibility of the loss of supremacy—in terms of wealth, privilege, prestige, power; the awful thought of a magnificent affluence threatened with collapse, if ever the African should rise, throw off his shackles, and achieve social and economic freedom.

Yet I cannot think there are many (if any) more spectacularly evil men in South Africa than anywhere else. It is not primarily brazen assault on life, limb or reputation (though, alas, not uncommon in a growingly police state) which leads men to say and do as the African minister did on Waterloo Station. Rather is it the chafing, abrasive impact of the tough scales of insensitivity encrusting the minds and attitudes of masses of ordinary respectable sinners, leaving red and raw the flesh of others they jostle out of their path on the highway of life.

Such insensitivity is lethal.

It is in the world of living organisms; of bodily cells. Ask any paraplegic. Talk to anybody who knows about leprosy and its treatment. Take away the sensitivity to pain, that God-sent sentinel, and the result can be disaster. The scalding water which is unfelt by the leprous fingers; the wound in the foot of the paraplegic, unfelt, unnoticed, untended . . . and ripe for infection; able to kill . . . such insensitivity can be lethal.

In her immensely moving book *Take My Hands*,[1] Dorothy Clark Wilson has a striking paragraph about the need for constant vigilance on the part of the paralysed, and refers to the kind of regimen which is happily unknown by normal mortals—but so vital a part of the life of the paraplegic.

Day after day, week after week, year after year, for as long as one should live, the patient, exacting ritual; examining the body thoroughly for reddened areas, using a hand mirror for back, hips, heels and elbows; bathing daily in warm water and soap, then rubbing lightly over the paralysed parts, applying powder where the skin was dry; using foam rubber pads to keep pressure off any part that shows signs of redness; making sure that no part was subjected to pressure for more than an hour; keeping the skin dry; treating every slightest abrasion as if it was a mortal wound. Monotonous, time-consuming routines, but for the paraplegic, a matter of life or death!

Mercifully, most of us know nothing of this hidden challenge, this danger lurking in the everyday, for those robbed of a tactile facility we take for granted. Let us pause—remember, imaginatively—and be deeply thankful.

Let us remember too the far greater peril, just as deeply concealed, fearful also in its potentiality for ruin, represented by loss of sensitivity in the realm of mind and spirit. In a neighbourhood-sized world, where men rub shoulders daily by the million with their fellow men, a world of endless intimate encounter, bland insensitivity to hurts, deprivation inflicted willingly on others, neither

[1] Hodder and Stoughton.

lessens the wound, nor its sad infected consequences. Insensitivity is merciless, and, in opposition to mercy, operates in precisely the reverse direction. It is twice cursed. It curses both the afflicter and the afflicted. We are members of one another. Your loving sensitivity or hard insensitivity inter-acts upon mine, to our mutual joy or sorrow. What we need, it seems, is some sort of insight, understanding, some inner fine re-honing of mind and outlook, enabling us to cut cleanly through the tough blunt callous of insensitivity: permitting us each one to look upon our neighbour, half a yard or half a world away, as a human being.

Which is where, perhaps, dinner at Simon's might offer a clue. From first to last, it is a study in sensitivity.

Look at the three characters involved in this unforgettable encounter. There are at least a couple of observations one can make, about each of them—the host, the disreputable woman gate-crasher, and our Lord, the honoured guest.

Ah, but *was* he an honoured guest? Hardly, from the evidence to hand. Every reader draws his own conclusions about Simon's reasons for inviting Jesus; but it's clear that the atmosphere at the dinner party couldn't possibly have been normal. It's pretty plain, in fact, that Simon had invited our Lord not as a fellow human being, but as an intriguing novelty. I see Simon as a scalp-hunter, a dilettante, a curious *avant-garde* Pharisee priding himself upon being 'with it' but certainly not 'of it' so far as the character of his unique guest was concerned. I fancy his aim was to scrutinize Jesus coolly at close range, to analyse, probe, quiz; to put himself in the position of being able to say at forthcoming Pharisaic fraternals, 'Well actually I had the man along to my place a while back . . . interesting fellow . . . picturesque character . . . a good deal of primitive shrewdness, and a real flair for words . . . nothing of real significance about him, of course . . .'

I think Simon wanted to exploit, not to entertain. To him, Jesus was, shall we say, something less than a human being. Certainly, something less than Simon.

And so, naturally, the normal courtesies could be dispensed with. No point in wasting good water for feet-washing—the man was essentially a peasant type who didn't go in for such niceties of civilized behaviour, anyway. Certainly he wouldn't be looking for a welcoming kiss . . . not after the things he was reputed to have said about Pharisees! And there'd be not the remotest need to offer the customary fragrant oil for his head . . . he wouldn't know what to do with it. He'd be far more at home if such frills were quietly ignored . . . get on with the job of eating, and talking . . . yes, of course, that was the best plan . . .

Doubtless Simon thought himself an enlightened sensible man as he carried his private assessment into public effect.

The two fairly obvious comments falling due about Simon can be summarized into a brief sentence.

He was most shrewdly sensitive to the assumed disabilities and failings of others; and oddly insensitive to his own.

Which, of course, is a fair description of the average, mediocre sinner, dull and stupid, in every age and clime, from South Africa to Surbiton; from Mississippi to Manchester.

This Pharisee was sensitive to the girl of the streets, as soon as she appeared. No unawareness here! He recognized her for what she was. Quick as a flash, he summed up the situation. His swift analysis, sure, self-confident, beguiled him to a fatuous conclusion as completely wide of the mark as possible. Pride rides every man for a fall, humiliating and ignominious. *This fellow . . . if he were a prophet . . . would know who this woman is . . . what sort she is . . . a sinner!*

Out of his bumbling unimagination Simon attributes the most crass insensitivity to the Lord of life. How stupid can you get? Answer—there's actually no limit to the formidable idiocy to which, self-critical faculties numbed, mentally hooked, and disabled, pride and prejudice can gently lead a man. It leads him to see things which aren't there, ignore things which *are*, and behave like a perfect fool. It clouds his perception and warps his judgement. It is quite, quite deadly.

Needless to say, our Lord knew the type. Every reader of the Gospels knows he put them under sharp scrutiny more than once. Here, perhaps, in Simon, is the prototype (there must have been at least one, in real life, somewhere, on whom the sadly astonished eyes of our Lord lit) of the Pharisee who prayed in the temple, a monstrous, invisible curtain stretched between himself and the penitent publican with whom he was rubbing shoulders. How swiftly Jesus sketches the outline of this self-righteous character, deeply touched by and sensitive to his own enormous good fortune; movingly grateful that he is not as other men— greedy, dishonest, adulterous—or, for that matter, like this wretched creature here beside him! The Pharisee of the parable was encapsuled in a super-texture insulation, a cocoon of self-conscious, self-centred, self-satisfied glee far removed from the joy of heaven over the sinner repenting by his side.

Or here, in Simon, is rich man Dives (who, with the Pharisee in the Temple, occurs—typically—in Luke). Dives was doubtless deeply appreciative, deeply sensitive to the splendid benefits life had conferred upon him. He remained massively insensitive however to the fact that a starving beggar lay at his gate. Lazarus was part of the landscape; a feature of the established order. It did not occur to Dives that anything could be done, should be done, to disturb the *status quo*. That outrageous insensitivity, you may recall, proved lethal to Dives in the end.

Of course, there's one real danger in looking like this at Simon, Dives, and Co. It may blind us to our blood relationship with them. We are first cousins. We may conceivably overlook the fact, as we pass judgement on them, that the grace of God apart, we ourselves fit their role like a glove. It is we ourselves, well clothed in pride but stripped of true love, whom we see mirrored in all these unlovely, unfeeling characters—until and unless by grace we have been enabled to move on; to fill a second, more dramatic, role: the woman who wept. To get to the heart of this matter of sensitivity and insensitivity, we have to take her part.

Every woman is born for love. So is every man, come to that. This poor soul, like many a million others, men and women alike, might have clutched feverishly at any and every splash of colour by the roadside of life, in case she missed anything on the way. So, she had gathered weeds as well as blossoms. She needed not men, but a man. A man to love; a man to love her, truly, deeply, not only to desire her, but, in possessing her, also to cherish her. Her need, like that of every man and woman, was of someone to whom she could give herself with that self-forgetful, self-fulfilling rapture and abandonment which all truly loving wives and husbands know, in the providence of God: a bliss which brings heaven and earth together.

But something had gone wrong; hideously wrong. She had earned not love, but contempt. She'd been tricked and trapped. And who knew, in any case, the temptations and pressures which had surrounded her, in earlier days? Who knew if she had ever had, in fact, any real chance at all to escape the net in which now she was helplessly caught? And who, in any case, cared? Certainly not Simon.

Now, she was a poor, broken thing, lusted after but never loved; contemptuously kicked around; a creature, a tool, at best a plaything; no longer a human being, in the eyes of others. To act the role of lover when you know full well what you are giving and receiving is an appalling, odious sham; to go drearily through the motions of love with an ache in your heart, and shame still trying fitfully to exercise some healing smart on your deadened mind . . . when all the time, deep down, you are hungry still for love—pure, vital, fulfilling . . . this is hell. The sort of hell which can turn your life by day into an intermittent haunting nightmare of bitter regret: in which the worst pain perhaps is an intolerable longing for something you know you have so deeply—perchance unwittingly—forfeited.

And if by chance (which afterwards you could recognize as an astounding act of providence) you had happened upon a real Man, resplendent in both virility and virtue, toughness and tenderness, whose words and deeds seemed instinct with life, fire and unsoiled innocence . . . who spoke compellingly of God, and love, of forgiveness, life, and joy, when your heart was heavy and you loathed your own body for what you had accustomed it to do . . . why then, it could be that you might come to feel a strange, unearthly compulsion to follow such a Man, simply to be near him, for the wondrous sense of healing joy-and-pain His presence afforded. You *could* be starting out, hardly aware of it at first, on a new kind of experience, a new way of life. You could at last be opening up again a pathway you had thought overgrown forever—the way back to sensitivity, to inner change—to become once more so alive to the ugliness of your life, that you could at some point resist no longer this Man's unspoken recall to beauty, newness of life; healed, restored, forgiven. Sometime, somewhere, you might simply break down . . . Your so long suppressed sense of guilt and shame, secret grief and unutterable loneliness, your agony of longing and yearning and not having—your anguished disappointment in all the men you'd known twisting inside you like a dagger—all these might combine finally to build up a

112

torrent of wild emotion which cascaded out, uncontrollable, leaving you utterly spent, yet open at last to receive the word of release and relief, the word of forgiveness and deep renewal.

Did it happen like this, to the woman, during dinner at Simon's?

I think so.

But the point is, it took the presence of Jesus to arouse, to sensitize her to the point of surrender—real surrender, of mind, of spirit, in which, for once, the banks of normal self-control were breached worthily.

The encounter, like so many others in the Gospels, was a symbol as well as a story: a symbol of the supreme role of the Son of God, Lord of Life. One way or another, what happened to the woman of the streets, happened to others too. Wherever he went, people were quickened, sensitized, as never before. They reacted swiftly, astonishingly, to the potency of his presence. From him radiated a sort of spiritual magnetic field. Men and women about him reacted often in astounding fashion to it. They felt something of his divine life seeking entrance to their own souls.

He told stories which reflected perfectly his own inmost heart of love, and that of the God with whom he was at one: about scapegrace sons, for instance, either wilful, headstrong, or intolerably self-righteous; and their father, with splendid discretion yet loving candour, showing the sort of merciful sensitivity which aimed to bring them back to their senses once again.

With splendid instinct he knew when to rebuke—but always without venom—and when to encourage; when to cheer, and when to challenge. He was intensely alive and aware of people—an awareness not of advantage to be gained, but blessing to be bestowed—or already claimed. He even knew, for instance, when 'power had gone out of him' as a woman in great distress and embarrassment,

113

touched him in the crowd, faith in her heart. 'My daughter, your faith has cured you,' he said tranquilly. 'Go in peace.'[1] It was entirely characteristic.

It happened in similar fashion, to the glad ending of the shame felt by a miserable man squatting in the branches of a wayside tree. A successful, self-made man: but a wretched little failure in his own heart of hearts, a twister, a bully. Upon him Jesus casts the same renewing, sensitizing, spell. Zaccheus fairly tumbles down from his perch in his haste to get closer. As he does so, his past begins to slough off him. He comes under the astounding influence. New life begins to take shape.

'Here and now, sir,' he says fervently. 'I give half my possessions to charity; and if I have cheated anyone, I am ready to repay him four times over.'[2] It was one of those moments of pure joy for the Master of life, coming to seek and save what had been lost.

Even when people resisted this deep sensitizing challenge of the Christ, they could not deny its self-authenticating truth and intensity. The rich young ruler, steeling himself against the direct call to discipleship, went away 'with a heavy heart',[3] knowing in his bones he had taken a disastrously wrong step. He retreated from the atmosphere of heaven, generated by Jesus, in which he could have found the new life he sought. He went away, awakened but unresponsive: a haunted man.

It's significant that alone among the people he mixed with, the religious establishment, Pharisees and scribes, lawyers and elders, remained impervious to the radiant power of his presence. They had insulated themselves in the brassy armour of impenetrable pride, unshakeably confident that they enjoyed already the whole truth and nothing but. They needed no more. They could learn no more. They snapped down the vizor of their self-esteem whenever he drew near, and glared out at him from narrow slits. They angrily derided him, one feels, as a

[1] Luke 9:48.   [2] Luke 19:8.   [3] Matt. 19:22.

ludicrous self-protective exercise as much as anything.

Yet hardly had the Gospel of the Resurrection begun to make its impact on men before even the establishment began to capitulate; symbolized in that strict and particular Pharisee Paul, who found himself arrested by the Lord of Life and provided by him with a new type of loving sensitivity so powerful, so novel, he was moved to describe it as a new creation of the Holy Spirit. Could anything else, could anything less, be responsible for turning his life inside out in such a thoroughgoing manner? What but the gracious invasion of God-in-Christ himself, could have turned Paul into such a red hot revolutionary citizen of God's commonwealth, from the lifelong and proudly cherished inheritance of a stiff-necked Jew, arrogantly glad to thank God daily, in his morning prayer, that he had been born neither Gentile, slave, nor woman?

'Through faith you are all sons of God in union with Christ Jesus,' he writes in exultation to the Galatians. 'You have all put on Christ as a garment. There is no such thing as Jew and Greek, slave and freeman, male and female; for you are all one person in Christ Jesus.'[1]

It was incredible, but true. A new breed of men had appeared; and will never die out. Men with eyes wide open, hearts gentle and strong, sensitive to the guidance and power alike of the Holy Spirit; men able to see and treat every other man as a human being, equally beloved, a royal son of the Father, with no rights not equally and joyously shared with all men everywhere.

One question only, of course, remains.

Are we in their number?

Are we as yet thick-skinned? Hard and insensitive? Or tender to the touch of others' needs, the anguish and the frailty of those about us, the cry of the beset and broken victims?

[1] Gal. 3:26–28.

You will save yourself infinite time and trouble, if you allow the natural insulation of self to harden and thicken over the years: if you remain at a safe distance from the Lord of Life.

Draw near and expose yourself penitently, however, in all your hard and graceless insensitivity, to his presence, and the miracle begins . . . with a new—but healing—smart, as the old Adam is skinned away, and the new man in Christ begins to appear. Indifference gives way to interest; contempt, to concern; sloth and self-satisfaction, to loving self-sacrifice. And with the change, both joy and travail: the joy of communion with the Lord of Love, who himself for the joy that was set before him endured the cross, despising the shame; and the travail of those who for the sake of the Kingdom of Christ have counted everything else but loss.

From one dinner-party to another—at which a chattering woman guest dropped a brick which thudded heavily into the conversation.

'Tell me,' she said confidentially to the man seated next to her, 'do you happen to know who that rather funny-looking man is, over in the corner?'

Her companion nodded, a trifle stiffly.

'I do indeed,' he said dryly. 'He's my brother.'

There was an awful pause. The unfortunate lady cast around desperately for something to retrieve the situation. At length—

'Of course!' she trilled breathlessly. 'How silly of me not to have seen the resemblance!'

To whom shall we liken ourselves in this study in sensitivity? Where do we find the resemblance?

In Simon?
In the woman?
In the Christ?

8) Pentecost: What *can* this mean?

IF there's one thing certain about Whitsuntide, it's this: that many average modern Christians, if they take the trouble to think about the festival at all, most certainly echo the honest bewilderment of the first eyewitnesses who watched the apostles tumble out into the Jerusalem street, that first Christian day; who turned to each other, 'all amazed and perplexed', as Luke reports, and said, 'What can this mean?'[1]

They had ample excuse for their bewilderment, those cosmopolitans from Mesopotamia, Cappadocia, Pontus, Asia, Egypt, Rome, and goodness knows where else, who made up the milling crowd packing the narrow thoroughfare in the brilliant morning sunshine; drawn together by the hubbub these eleven characters were making, who had just cascaded out into the open-air from their prayer meeting, bawling their heads off, clearly convulsed with the most tremendous emotions. The onlookers could catch but a word or two here and there (if they were words at all) above the general din.

'What *can* this mean?' asked some, gaping. There was at least one ready answer—'They've been drinking!'

Which down-to-earth reaction probably acted as a cold sponge on the minds of the ecstatic disciples. One imagines the leader of the band climbing to his feet, wiping his eyes, opening his lungs, and trying again—this time successfully—to get his message across in plain terms.

[1] Acts 2:12.

117

'Nonsense!' he cries. 'Why, it's only nine in the morning. Who's had time to get drunk at this time of day? No—this is what we've been expecting! It's God's Spirit at work—he's poured it out upon us! It's to happen to everybody—as you've heard the prophet said of old—so that young men shall see visions, old men dream dreams! No-one's to be missed out!—not even household slaves, men, women alike! The day of the Lord—the great, resplendent day is coming!—and everybody who calls on the name of the Lord shall be saved!'

By which time, he was getting into his stride.

'Men of Israel, listen to me'—his voice belled out—'I speak of Jesus of Nazareth, a man singled out by God and made known to you through miracles, portents and signs, which God worked among you through him, as you well know. When he had been given up to you . . . you used heathen men to crucify and kill him. But God raised him to life again, setting him free from the pangs of death, because it could not be that death should keep him in its grip.'

And on he went; clear, confident, convincing. It was one of the most important 'firsts' in the history of the world; the first time a follower of Jesus Christ, Son of God and Saviour, invested with the power that had been his Lord's, boldly proclaimed his faith. The event was a sensation—and a success. 'In these and many other words', says Luke, recording the occasion, 'he pressed his case and pleaded with them: "Save yourselves", he said, "from this crooked age." Then those who accepted his word were baptized, and some three thousand were added to their number that day.'[1]

The Christian community had been launched. The day of Pentecost had run its course. The world revolution had begun.

But to us today . . . what *can* this mean?

[1] Acts 2:41.

118

Now let's be clear. I'm not putting the question as if it was a real mystery; an unfathomable conundrum. It's nothing of the sort. There's a clear, cogent answer to it.

But the startling first few minutes of what we might call the Christian campaign certainly were mystifying. They'd have been a mystery to anybody. Admittedly, the atmosphere in the capital, this festival day, was one of intense religious excitement and fervour. If you get masses of people crowded together, sharing such a mood, spontaneous eruptions of enthusiasm and rapture can be expected. All the same, what happened to them, in sight of the onlookers, must have been baffling. To see a group of grown men stumbling about, shouting incoherently, clearly caught in the grip of some tremendous, indescribable, spiritual experience which had gripped and shaken them to the depths of their beings—why, it was enough to make anybody stand and stare in blank amazement.

The crowd's perplexity was perfectly understandable. We have less excuse.

Perhaps the real stumbling block to our modern minds rests in the account of these first few minutes: first while the disciples are at prayer, and then out in the open air, just before Peter becomes spokesman, and delivers his first impassioned Christian challenge.

For a start, the audio-visuals of the Pentecostal experience are in such bizarre contrast say to those of the other great events in the Christian calendar: notably Christmas and Easter. Sheep, shepherds, stars, wise men, new born babes, even angelic hosts—all these are imaginable, meaningful, clear. So are the far grimmer pictures of the Passion—the arrest, the trial, the last indelible scenes on Gibbet Hill; together with the lively record of a risen Lord, and of despair turned to deliverance.

But what are we moderns to make of the hurricane wind effects, the tongues like flames of fire, resting on

119

each of the disciples, at prayer on the day of Pentecost? What unmistakable message comes crystal clear at the sound of the disciples starting to talk—so the record asserts—in foreign languages they hadn't had to go to the trouble of learning? What relevance has this sort of happening, taken at its face value, for modern men in search of reality and salvation?

And so, timidly—or lazily?—posing such obvious questions, and refusing to stir far in search of any answer, we remain as confused as the onlookers of old. But there is a difference. We remain confused. They didn't. Their minds were clear quite soon. So can ours be, however, if we really want to find the answer to the question they posed. I'm convinced the difficulties modern Christians feel about the meaning of Pentecost aren't nearly as solid or vast as they seem to be. They can be resolved.

How do we get at the truth?

In the first place, by letting the events speak for themselves. Not just the dramatic birth pangs, as we might describe them, when the fire fell, and the disciples struggled into action. Those few moments are enthralling—but in the long run, as unimportant as the actual spasms of a mother giving birth to a child—very compelling at the time, yet speedily forgotten and of no significance afterwards. You simply must look, and look hard, at what happened before and after those hectic moments when the disciples were so dramatically 'under the influence', if you want to make sense of Pentecost. You have to see Whitsuntide in its proper setting, to appreciate its meaning. Stand too close, for too long, and you get the events out of focus. Stand well back for a minute or two. Take in the bigger picture. New light may well shine, as you do.

Retrace as clearly as you can, the steps of the disciples, right from the time they first encountered Jesus, to the day of Pentecost.

120

Swiftly, compellingly, they had fallen under the spell of a man who spoke and acted as did no man they had ever met before. He had no power, no prestige, no credentials; no friends at court, no privilege, no status. But he stood invested with an awesome power and authority which enthralled them. When he spoke, they knew they were hearing the truth. He stretched out his hands, lifted up his voice, and the sick and lame received new strength and healing. No man could deny the extraordinary power which flowed from him. The stiffnecked and arrogant fiercely rejected him. Yet whether a man blessed the name of Jesus or snarled 'he has a devil!' he could not deny that through this man surged a truly marvellous power, which his followers unhesitatingly recognized as the Spirit of God. He yoked words and deeds in a way which led some seriously to think that Elijah, or another of the giants of old, was reborn in him. But to those nearest him, even this fell far short of the stupendous reality forcing itself on their astonished minds.

Peter spoke for the rest, at a moment of unflawed insight, when he confessed that this Jesus, whom they gladly called Master and Lord, was in fact the long awaited Messiah, the Son of the living God—the embodiment of God's very presence and purpose and power, his goodness and his love, standing clear for all men to see.

Now: try to enter into the disciples' experience, as the final months sped by, and the clouds of implacable hatred, never far distant, thickened and lowered. That he should fail was unthinkable. The Messiah was the triumphant conqueror, born to usher in the kingly reign of God, the reign of righteousness and peace. And yet . . .

And yet, as events hurried on, his enemies grew more intent than ever on his destruction. At the last, the expected glorious deliverance, which without doubt the anxious disciples were expecting, simply didn't happen. They saw their beloved Lord, the Master whose words and works had surged out with such power and authority, broken, beaten to his knees. His humiliation and torment was bitter and complete. So, in a different way, was theirs. We are familiar with the story; too familiar, perhaps. Try hard to see it as the twelve saw it; to feel as they felt. The events of Thursday to Saturday of that first Passion-tide must have come as an appalling, paralysing shock. They were quite demoralized; men whose hope and faith had been blasted to atoms; for whom life had with awful abruptness, ceased to have any meaning. They were, in a terrifying sense, lost. No wonder one of them, for whatever immediate reasons, committed suicide. The rest must have felt likewise on the verge of insanity.

This is not to overplay the drama. Unless the Gospels are giving us a wholly inadequate picture of Jesus and the story of his passion, what lesser emotions can have swept through these volatile Galileans, as they contemplated the disaster of Calvary?

Then, with hardly a pause, came the violent event of Easter. Violent, because without warning, it catapulted them from the abyss of total despair to the dizziest heights of joy. Anguish turned to exultation. They became suddenly, completely aware that their Master was alive. They were as sure of it as they had previously been sure he was dead; a battered corpse in a stone tomb. But what did this incredible reversal of fortune mean? What *now*, was to happen?

It is vital to try very hard to enter into the experience of the disciples during these critical days following Easter and to answer the question just posed, if you want to make sense of Pentecost. You simply must ask what they were thinking, feeling, what sense they were making, of the certainties which now were theirs. He had lived among them, and they had beheld his glory: the glory, John was later to say, as of the only begotten Son of the Father, full of grace and truth. They had truly known and believed him to be the Way, the Truth, and the Life of

God. He had opened up the gates of understanding. They knew his message meant the splintering of the barriers of self and pride, the reconciliation of men with God, and so of man with man; and they knew it was an imperishable message. It had embedded itself in their lives. Now, he remained its enduring symbol—a living Lord, not a lost leader. They must have sensed, irresistibly, that, under his lordship, the Good News that all men could and should live as loving neighbours in a world which still waited to be transformed into the family of God, *must continue to be proclaimed*. The task of Jesus must be sustained—*through them*. Certainly, whichever way you look at it; whatever unfocussed truths their minds had not yet managed to sharpen and comprehend, *they must have known there was a vital future for them. The risen Lord was in command still.* The road had not ended. The way ahead for the moment was shrouded. But *it was there*: of this they must have been perfectly certain. All they could do for the time being was to peer eagerly, expectantly, into the unknown, and wait for . . .

Ah yes, that's the question. Wait for . . . what? Why, for the next step to be revealed; for something to happen which would (to use commonplace language) trigger off the new stage of the Christian movement. They would be enabled to pick up from where they had so abruptly left off, fleeing in horror and panic, from the Garden. They would press on with the selfsame message of one whom now they knew to be invisible but alive, among them for evermore. But when, and how, would the great new forward movement begin?

The Gospel record offers us solid clues encouraging the kind of reconstruction just attempted. Luke, both in his Gospel and the early verses of Acts, drops plain hints that the disciples were awaiting 'power from on high'— power to launch them into action. What more apt than that the signal would be given at Jerusalem? The move-

123

ment would begin again in the very place where, apparently, it had been stopped dead.

So: unless you are prepared to dimiss the record both of the Gospels and the Acts as thoroughly untrustworthy—which really isn't sensible—you begin to see just how this six week period from Easter to Whitsuntide fits into the unfolding pattern. Simple men don't get over a succession of tremendous emotional shocks in a day or two. They need time, plenty of time, for what can reasonably be called emotional and mental recuperation; the building up of new attitudes, new perspectives, new certainties. The disciples were able bit by bit now to recollect, in the light of the resurrection, much that they recalled with wonder from the past—the words he had spoken time and again about his coming torment, death, and rising again. They needed time to rethink, basically, completely; to see how gloriously fitting it was that the Messiah *could* suffer and die, and still remain conquering Son of God. They needed time to search the scriptures; to make sense of the facts as now they knew them. To use modern shorthand for their experience, they needed most urgently, a reorientation period.

This is exactly what the weeks between Easter and Pentecost provided.

It is not improbable—it is, on the contrary, most necessary to imagine the disciples steadily becoming ever more joyously sure of themselves, as they read the scriptures, prayed, and sensed the dawning of new certainty about the meaning of his triumph, and their future role. We might without sentimentality call this first Easter-Whitsuntide period a unique spiritual honeymoon, shared between Christ and his newly betrothed disciples, the Church in embryo; a time of blissful content, of intensely private, deeply fruitful preparation for the rigours of the mission to which they were so soon to be exposed; to

124

which they were about to commit without stint the rest of their lives.

But waiting periods must come to an end. That end is often marked decisively. What was needed, if we may look at the situation from the human angle, was a special stimulus; an occasion which would cause them to spring back into action—as the arrest in the Garden had caused them so tragically to dart away in terror.

What more likely, what more entirely appropriate, than the next great special festival of the Jewish Year— Pentecost.

Is it not fitting that what did happen, happened how, when, and where it did?

Pentecost was a harvest festival. The first of the barley crop was offered as a token of thankfulness. Vast crowds thronged the capital. It was a time of joy and fervour. What more natural, more inevitable, on the view just outlined, than that the fervent zeal of the eager crowds, shared we may be sure by the disciples, should build up and burst out, in their case, into such a rapture of ecstasy that the banks of normal restraint were dramatically breached? As they prayed, knowing that they were in fact soon to receive the inner power they needed to begin again, with their risen Lord; knowing he was about them; knowing that the world awaited them; knowing they had a faith to declare—what happened? Suddenly, mind and heart, conviction and experience, fused together in a moment of overwhelming spiritual glory, of incandescent brilliance: a moment of fire and thunder.

Luke, writing calmly from a safe distance in time, does his best to describe it—and a valiant best it is, too. None of us would have got anywhere near the heart of the event as does the artless record of Acts two— attempting to express the frankly inexpressible. No wonder Luke had to fall back on picture language. You might as well try to mend a wristwatch with gloves on as

125

use words accurately to describe the first moments of the first Pentecost: this mighty outflowing of the Spirit of God into the hearts of waiting men.

All that the disciples knew was that they were in the grip of an overwhelming spiritual power, possessing them whole and entire, flinging them about, driving them out into the street, there for the time being to mouth sounds which made glorious sense to them, if not to anyone else, and which somehow expressed the unspeakable glory and wonder of the certainty that the time was—*now*! It had happened! They were aware of one thing. The promise was fulfilled. The tide of understanding and faith had been flowing strongly, silently, imperceptibly, ever since they had become aware that Jesus had triumphed over the grave. Now, the Pentecostal festival provided a narrow channel through which the waters rose to pour out dramatically in the sight of all. The power had come! The message must be unleashed. They must begin again in the power of the Holy Spirit—the presence and energy of the risen Lord—*now*!

It's small wonder that for the first unbearable moments of shattering spiritual intensity and awareness, only broken ejaculations and sounds of ecstasy came from their lips; or that these were taken later on and reverently enlarged into something magical, by people re-telling the story (and understandably anxious to impress) so that what was a tumultuous, supercharged emotional experience producing the language of ecstasy—a not uncommon phenomenon in moments of intense rapturous spiritual awareness—becomes an ability to speak not 'in tongues', but in *foreign* tongues. Only a modest degree of imagination is required to see how this understandable but distracting bit of embroidery crept into the record. Don't let it distract you now. Don't let it blind you to the inner truth of the event of Pentecost. Look beyond it, into the heart of the happening.

126

The first moments of the Pentecostal experience are a fitting, inevitable, dramatic prologue; *nothing more*. Stay with them, concentrate on them, and you will be as misled as those who scoffed contemptuously that these men had been drinking.

Try, as we have done, to live through the experience of the disciples, during the weeks prior to the festival, and the far deeper truth starts to appear.

And what is that truth?

Why—that Pentecost was the spectacular, but gloriously understandable end of the beginning; the start of a new age; symbolized in the new community that came to birth that day—a community invested with a new quality of living, a new power from on high.

When you stop as we have done, to think carefully, imaginatively through the undoubted experiences of the disciples, between Easter and Pentecost, you see clearly at least one thing. It ought to clear a great deal of confusion from the mind of any seeker after the truth and meaning of the festival. It is that Pentecost was not an unexpected, unheralded, incomprehensible bolt from the spiritual blue. On the contrary, given the basic assumptions of the death and resurrection of Jesus, and the meaning of his ministry, you could say that Pentecost, or something like it, was necessary; even predictable.

When you go on to look at what immediately followed— using the record of the next few chapters of Acts as guide—such convictions are strengthened.

I am convinced that if every churchgoer would spend as much as ten minutes before church on Whit Sunday, reading for his inspiration and delight the first five chapters of Acts, a great deal of the uncertainty and confusion he may feel about the festival, would vanish like morning mist when the sun gets up.

What pictures do we see, from these chapters, springing freshly before our eyes?

A succession of strange eccentric happenings, remote and unintelligible, performed by a band of spiritual weirdies, bewildering those who witnessed them?

Nothing of the sort.

These chapters—and indeed, a good many that follow—are alive with a surging new life which enabled ordinary men and women to perform the most extraordinary, redeeming actions: words and works of clear, compelling Christlike power and compassion. After the great response to Peter's first Gospel message, the others joined in. This fresh 'outpouring of the Spirit' continued and spread. It drew together those who shared it. 'A sense of awe was everywhere', said Luke; and 'many marvels and signs' were done through the apostles' ministry. A joyous, spontaneous share-and-share-alike community sprang up. Those within it found themselves enjoying a new revolutionary kind of family spirit, in which it was unthinkable that anybody should go short. They shared their meals, and their worship, 'with unaffected joy'. What a lovely description of the quality of this society just born! It stirs the heart to read of the way in which the Gospel broke upon the world, and what it started to achieve. The world saw lives charged with the spirit of love and caring; cripples healed; men challenged to the depths of their beings to begin again, a new life, with Christ at the centre . . . a new life which incidentally—and inevitably—leads the apostles almost at once into head-on collision with the establishment, and for the selfsame reasons which led their risen Lord to his death.

The spirit-charged apostles are the champions of universal love—at any price. They are renewed, resourceful, confident, filled with joy. They cannot be shut up or shut down. They find words to argue their case. They bear about them the signs of the same Spirit in which their Lord stood invested, in the days of his flesh; and, amazing fellows, their newfound faith and strength are proof against the fury of their still hardened adversaries. After a flogging, Peter and the rest of the apostles go out from the enraged Council with bleeding backs (I quote again from Luke) 'rejoicing that they had been found worthy to suffer indignity for the sake of the Name. And every day they went steadily on with their teaching in the temple and in private houses, telling the good news of Jesus the Messiah'.

Why do we feel so moved by this invigorating account? Let J. B. Phillips give us his answer, in the preface to his own translation of Acts—a preface itself inspiring and enheartening. He says:

The reader is stirred because he is seeing Christianity, the real thing, in action for the first time in human history. The new-born Church, as vulnerable as any human child, having neither money nor influence, nor power in the ordinary sense, is setting forth joyfully and courageously to win the pagan world for God, through Christ. The young Church, like all young creatures, is appealing in its simplicity and single-heartedness. Here we are seeing the Church in its first youth, valiant and unspoiled—a body of ordinary men and women joined in an unconquerable fellowship never before seen on this earth.[1]

It's against this reality that the colourful chaos, the unfamiliar emotional paroxysm of the first moments of the first Whitsuntide experience, have to be set. The tongues of fire, the rushing mighty wind, and the first moments of unintelligible ecstasy have their counterpart one way or another in mountain top human experiences of many kinds. But when thoughtfully looked at, they aren't nearly so offputting and inexplicable as our lazy minds would at a casual glance suggest. And the cogent testimony of what then followed, is as persuasive, as disturbing in its challenge, as anything could be.

[1] *The Young Church in Action*, Fontana, p. 11.

Let's be clear about Whitsuntide. The fact is that the meaning of the festival isn't really cloudy at all. It's most disconcertingly clear. It is the record of what happened when men stood willing to be possessed, used by God as he had come to them through the risen Lord Jesus. It is the record of men willing to be energized by his limitless invisible power, investing them with superhuman Christlike reserves of inner authority, joy, compassion.

Until then, the apostles had reflected but fitfully, if at all, the strength and spirit of their Master.

Now, things were changed. The investiture at Pentecost meant that henceforth they stood garbed in his majesty, his humility, his fearless, total concern for the Kingdom of God. It happened as the proper, splendid climax to their strenuous years of apprenticeship.

This is how it has happened a million times down the short Christian centuries separating them from us privileged to stand in the line of succession today.

You have met some of the latter day apostles, filled with the Spirit? Their lives have touched yours? You have seen in them, as men did of old, a power, a splendid confidence, a loving kindness, a sacrificial valour which you could only describe as 'Christlike'? You have asked 'What can this mean?'

So have I. And if I had not encountered such Spirit-filled folk, if I had not seen the results of Pentecost in the lives of men and women, modern apostles who touched my life for good, through whom Christ spoke to me, I should not now be speaking to you. We do not need to be told that this is the final point of the whole story.

See how great a flame aspires,
Kindled by a spark of grace!
Jesu's love the nations fires,
Sets the kingdoms on a blaze.
To bring fire on earth He came;
Kindled in some hearts it is:

130

> *O that all might catch the flame,*
> *All partake the glorious bliss!*

It hovers near, that flame, this Whitsun morning. It waits to alight—on you, perhaps?